FORMER LAPD RESERVE OFFICE
HON. STEVE

M000237649

BLUE LIVES IN JEOPARDY

WHEN THE BADGE BECOMES THE TARGET

CAREER PROSECUTOR & OFFICE HISTORIAN
ROBERT SCHIRN

BLUE LIVES IN JEOPARDY: When the Badge Becomes the Target

© Steve Cooley & Robert Schirn. ALL RIGHTS RESERVED.

Authored by Steve Cooley and Robert Schirn

Published by TitleTown Publishing | TEN23 MEDIA
Green Bay, Wisconsin
www.titletownpublishing.com

No part of this book may be reproduced in any form or by any means, electronic or me-
chanical, including photocopying, recording, taping, or by any storage and retrieval
system, without the written permission of Steve Cooley, Robert Schirn, or TitleTown Publishing.

Interior design by TitleTown Publising
Cover design by TitleTown Publising
Cover photo © TitleTown Publishing. ALL RIGHTS RESERVED

Publisher's note:
This book, including names, characters, places, and incidents, is based on true events. Some names and identifying
details may have been changed for privacy reasons. The authors alone bear responsibility for any remaining errors
in the text, which are wholly unintentional.

ISBN (hardcover): 978-1-949042-14-6
ISBN (paperback): 978-1-949042-15-3
This title is also available in electronic and audiobook formats.

PUBLISHER'S CATALOGING-IN-PUBLICATION DATA
Cooley, Steve; Schirn, Robert
BLUE LIVES IN JEOPARDY/ COOLEY & SCHIRN
1st edition. Green Bay, WI: TitleTown Publishing, c2019.

Proudly Printed in the United States of America
10 9 8 7 6 5 4 3 2 1

"It's not how these officers died that made them heroes, it's how they lived."

Vivian Eney Cross, Survivor

CONTENTS

PROLOGUE

COMMENTARY OF STEVE COOLEY

INTRODUCTION

BLUE LIVES IN JEOPARDY: When the Badge Becomes the Target is the second book of a trilogy I co-authored with Robert (Bob) Schirn involving the deaths of law enforcement officers in Los Angeles County. The first book in our series, *Blue Lives Matter: In the Line of Duty* (hereafter referred to as "Book One"), was released in the fall of 2017 and received national and international praise.

Bob and I began collaborating in 2014 and discussed writing a book examining the line-of-duty deaths suffered by law enforcement officers. We were career prosecutors familiar with the cases prosecuted by the Los Angeles County District Attorney's Office involving those deaths. My experience as a reserve police officer and as a three-term elected District Attorney, and Bob's status as a career prosecutor and office historian, gave us access to information and documents not available to the general public. We identified over twenty-five cases that would be appropriate for the books.

We had several purposes in mind in writing these books. First, these books memorialize and honor the law enforcement officers who have given their lives in service to their community and to their profession. Second, there is a "Lessons Learned" segment in each chapter intended to make officers aware of dangerous situations and to promote their safety. In this regard, the books serve as a training manual for law enforcement officers. A third purpose is to emphasize the importance of a strong working relationship between investigators and prosecutors in solving these crimes and putting together the best possible case for criminal prosecution. Prosecuting agencies should maintain special units or assign specially trained prosecutors to assist in the investigation and prosecution of cases involving the murder and serious assault of law enforcement officers.

BOOK ONE

We chose eight cases to comprise the eight chapters for Book One. A major theme for Book One was that "When it comes to killing a peace officer, we do not forgive, we do not forget, we do not give up." In other words, law enforcement agencies are especially diligent in investigating, solving, and prosecuting cases involving the death of a law enforcement officer. Book One included chapters involving the murder of two officers solved over forty years later; a successful retrial after the murder conviction was reversed by the California Supreme Court; and changing the law to extradite a cop-killer who fled to Mexico to avoid prosecution.

BLUE LIVES IN JEOPARDY:
When the Badge Becomes the Target

A major theme in Book Two is a very disturbing trend for law enforcement officers. More and more officers have been targeted for assassination merely because they are wearing a police uniform and/or performing a police function. In some cases, the officer was ambushed or taken by surprise with his weapon still in his holster. In chapters three through eight of this book the victim officers were shot before they could draw their weapon. The most glaring example of an outright assassination was the murder of CHP Officer Thomas Steiner, who was shot by a sixteen-year-old who wanted to impress a street gang he wished to join.

LESSONS LEARNED

A valuable and instructive component in Book One was the segment on "Lessons Learned" that appeared at the end of each chapter. Former LAPD Captain Greg Meyer is one of the nation's foremost experts on police tactics and officer safety, having lectured and provided expert testimony on these topics throughout the country over the years. He has again provided his expertise and insights in the "Lessons Learned" segments in each chapter of this book. These segments can hopefully assist officers in recognizing dangerous situations and enhance officer safety.

CAPOS: Crimes Against Peace Officers Section

In 1980, the Los Angeles County District Attorney's Office created the Crimes Against Peace Officers Section (CAPOS), a special unit consisting of highly skilled prosecutors to handle cases involving the murder and serious assault of police officers. Every chapter in Books One and Two that involves the murder or serious injury to a peace officer after 1980 has been prosecuted by a deputy district attorney assigned to CAPOS. The remarkable success enjoyed by CAPOS can be attributed to the outstanding investigative efforts by law enforcement and the legal skills of the prosecutors assigned to CAPOS.

GANG VIOLENCE

It is estimated there are over 400 street gangs in Los Angeles County with approximately 45,000 members. Many of the gangs use violence to maintain control over their turf and the lucrative narcotics trade in their territory. Crimes of violence, including murder, are common occurrences between rival gang members in Los Angeles County.

The larger police agencies in Los Angeles County have created special units of officers to combat gang violence. Smaller agencies will often participate in regional task forces to suppress violent and criminal gang activity.

An adversarial relationship often exists between the police officers investigating gangs and the gang members. As a result, some gang members will shoot at police officers with little or no provocation. The great majority of shooting deaths of police officers in Los Angeles County since 1996 were committed by gang members.

In this book, Chapters 5-8 involve a background of gang violence or gang influence. Four of the shooters were in fact gang members and the fifth shooter shot the officer to impress the street gang that he wished to join. None of the officers was even able to unholster his weapon before being taken by surprise or ambushed.

DEATH PENALTY IN CALIFORNIA

In 1972, the California Supreme Court voided the death penalty in California on the grounds that it constituted "cruel and unusual punishment." In 1978, the death penalty in California was restored by the voters pursuant to the initiative process.

Since the death penalty was reinstated, juries in California that have rendered judgment in cases involving the murder of a police officer have tended to favor a death sentence. In Book One, all seven defendants were convicted of first-degree murder and four received the death penalty. In this book, all eight defendants were convicted of murder, and in five cases the jury rendered a verdict of death (one defendant was a juvenile who was ineligible by law for a death sentence).

Despite the large number of cop killers on death row in California, none of them has been executed since the death penalty was reinstated in California in 1978. In fact, no one has been executed in California since 2006, as the courts have reviewed California's legal injection protocol as the means of execution. Any executions in California are unlikely in the foreseeable future as California Governor Gavin Newsom, in March 2019, declared a moratorium on the death penalty in California.

ACKNOWLEDGEMENTS

CO-AUTHOR BOB SCHIRN AND I firmly believe this book provides an important public service by demonstrating that law enforcement officers are dedicated public servants who place their lives at risk in protecting society on a daily basis. We are fortunate our partners at TitleTown Publishing, Owner and Publisher, Tracy Ertl and Chief Executive Officer, Travis Vanden Heuvel, share our vision. They have capably guided us through the complexities of book publishing and provided encouragement in the process.

Bob Schirn and I spoke to many individuals who investigated or prosecuted the cases set forth in this book. This included the prosecutors who handled these cases in court including Lowell Anger, Mark Arnold, James Ideman, Darren Levine, Sterling Norris, and Barbara Turner. They checked the chapters for accuracy and provided us with valuable insights, anecdotes, and information on each case.

Of the prosecutors who handled the cases described in this book, Mark Arnold deserves special mention. He has had three significant careers. He was a Los Angeles County Deputy Sheriff from 1972 to 1985. He went to law school at night, passed the state bar exam, and was a Los Angeles County Deputy District Attorney from 1985 to 1998. He was the prosecutor in two of the cases in this book – Chapter 3 involving the murders of Compton police officers Kevin Burrell and James MacDonald and Chapter 5 describing the murder of Pomona police officer Daniel Fraembs. Arnold convicted the defendants in both cases of first-degree murder, and both defendants received the death penalty. In 1998, Governor Pete Wilson appointed Mark Arnold to the bench; he has served as a judge of the Los Angeles Superior Court since then.

Former law enforcement officers who provided information and materials include Mark Lillienfeld, Tim Miley, Michael Thies, Delores Perales Scott, and Jimmy Trahin. The substantial contributions of retired LAPD Captain Greg Meyer, who provided the "Lessons Learned" segments in each chapter, have already been acknowledged.

Typing and computer services were provided by Joyce Irving, William Marcus, and Sylvia Nunez. My personal secretary and good friend Cathy Hawks placed the chapters in a manuscript form and did much of the typing and final editing. She's been wonderful.

Bob Schirn and I continue to receive the support and encouragement of our families in this project. I am indebted to my wife of forty-four years, Jana, and my children Michael and Shannon. Bob wants to express his thanks to his wife of over fifty years, Zanda, and his sons Brian and Jason. Brian is a head deputy with over twenty-five years with the District Attorney's Office.

Co-authors Bob Schirn and Steve Cooley

Co-author Bob Schirn and editor Cathy Hawks

Reserve LAPD Officer Steve Cooley with partner
Officer Jimmy Trahin circa 1975

Captain Greg Meyer

CHAPTER ONE

The Newhall Incident

California Highway Patrol

"Vehicle Stop Leads to Massacre"

April 5, 1970

INTRODUCTION

ON APRIL 5, 1970, after a vehicle stop in the Newhall area of Los Angeles County, four young California Highway Patrol officers were killed in a gun battle with two heavily armed career criminals. The sequential deaths of Officers Walter C. Frago, Roger D. Gore, James E. Pence, Jr., and George M. Alleyn occurred during a shootout which lasted less than five minutes. It is still the greatest loss of life of law enforcement officers during a vehicle stop in the history of law enforcement in the United States. The death of these four officers is often referred to as "The Newhall Incident."

All the officers were under twenty-five years of age at the time of their deaths. All four officers had been members of the California Highway Patrol for less than three years. These officers did not die in vain since "The Newhall Incident" resulted in a series of revisions of procedures during high-risk and felony vehicle stops.

THE CALIFORNIA HIGHWAY PATROL

The California Highway Patrol (CHP) was created in 1929 by legislation enacted by the California State Legislature and signed into law by Governor C. C. Young. The new law gave the CHP statewide authority to enforce traffic laws on county and state highways and, in fact, on any public road anywhere in the state. This responsibility to manage and regulate traffic to achieve safe, lawful, and efficient use of the highway transportation system remains the primary mission of the CHP.

Numerous additional functions have been added to the CHP's purview since 1929. Today's responsibilities include truck and bus inspections, air operations (both airplanes and helicopters), and vehicle theft investigation and prevention. The CHP has taken a leadership role in educating the public concerning driving safety issues (e.g., promoting use of

seat belts, car seats for young children, helmets for motorcyclists and bi-
cycle riders, and designated drivers). CHP officers also act as bailiffs for
the California Supreme Court and as security for State of California buildings.

With over 10,000 employees, the CHP is the largest state police agency in the United States. The department is comprised of uniformed
(sworn) and non-uniformed (unsworn) personnel, with uniformed personnel accounting for approximately seventy percent of the total staff.
Approximately two-thirds of the CHP's uniformed personnel are assigned
to patrol duties on roadways throughout the state. The CHP's remaining
uniformed personnel perform various non-patrol duties for the department.

THE VEHICLE STOP
Los Angeles County, California
April 5, 1970 – 11:37 p.m.

DISPATCH: *Unit 78-8, Newhall CHP.*

MOBILE UNIT: *Newhall 78-8, we're on the five-mile*
                            grade. Go ahead.

DISPATCH: *78-8, we have a reported brandishing of*
                            a weapon fifteen minutes ago. A red '64
                            Pontiac, Cal license Ocean, Sam, Yellow,
                            8-0-5, that's OSY805, southbound on
                            Highway 99 from Gorman area. The
                            driver threatened another driver with a
                            revolver.

MOBILE UNIT: *Newhall 78-8, 10-4. We copied and we'll*
                            watch for it.

This call was to result in the convergence of four young California Highway Patrol Officers and two hardened, career criminals. Ten hours later,

the four CHP officers had been shot to death, one suspect committed suicide, and the other suspect was in custody. One citizen made heroic efforts to assist the officers; another citizen had been pistol-whipped during the theft of his car; still another citizen was held hostage in his home for over four hours.

The incident began on April 5, 1970, at approximately 11:15 p.m. Jack Tidwell, an enlisted man with the United States Navy, and his wife were southbound on U.S. Highway 99 near the town of Gorman. Tidwell was in the high-speed lane next to the highway's center divider. As he approached the area known as Pyramid Rock, a northbound vehicle made a U-turn across the center divider into his path.

Tidwell was able to avoid a collision, after which he pulled alongside the vehicle, a red Pontiac, and his wife rolled down her window. Through the open passenger window, Tidwell yelled to the offending driver and lone occupant of the vehicle that he'd like to "kick his ass." Both vehicles came to a stop, and the driver of the Pontiac produced a handgun and called Mr. Tidwell a "smart ass." Mr. Tidwell saw a car's headlights in his rear-view mirror and told the man with the gun that the oncoming car was the California Highway Patrol. The driver motioned with his gun for the Tidwell car to leave. Jack Tidwell quickly drove off, and he and his wife made note of the color, make, and license number of the vehicle.

Eight miles south of where the incident had occurred, at Violin Canyon Road, the Tidwells stopped to use a pay telephone. There, Mrs. Tidwell called the CHP office to report what had happened while Mr. Tidwell watched to see if the red Pontiac passed. She provided a description of the incident and of the vehicle, including the license plate number. The Tidwells declined to sign a complaint since serviceman Tidwell was due back at Port Hueneme, where he was stationed.

It was at this point that dispatch contacted Unit 78-8 and described the incident and a description of the 1964 red Pontiac, including the license number. CHP Officers Walt Frago and Roger Gore in Unit 78-8 observed the vehicle southbound on Highway 99. The Pontiac turned off on Henry Mayo Drive and stopped in the driveway entrance for a Standard

Oil station and J's Restaurant. Unit 78-8 radioed that the vehicle was stopped at this location, and Unit 78-12 containing Officers James Pence and George Alleyn radioed that they would "be there in a minute" to provide backup.

THE OFFICERS
Unit 78-8

On the evening of April 5, 1970, CHP Unit 78-8 was driven by Officer Roger Gore with Officer Walt Frago as the passenger officer. Both men were in full uniform in a marked CHP cruiser.

Officers Gore and Frago had both recently celebrated their birthdays. Walt Frago turned twenty-three on December 22, 1969, and Roger Gore celebrated his twenty-third birthday less than two months later on February 17, 1970. Both men had been born and raised in Merced, California, and attended Merced High School, where they became best friends.

They joined the California Highway Patrol at the same time, and, in August 1968, they reported to the same CHP class in Sacramento. On December 12, 1968, they were both assigned to the CHP Newhall Station, where they worked as partners. For a short time, they transferred together as partners to the West Valley CHP station; they both returned to the Newhall station where they continued to work as partners in the same patrol unit.

Both Roger Gore and Walt Frago were married and lived a block apart in the City of Newhall. They drove to and from work together, and their wives were best friends.

Walt Frago and his wife Nikki had two daughters, Amorette, four, and Gabriela, three. Roger Gore was married to Valerie with whom he had an eighteen-month old daughter, Elyse.

Unit 78-12

On the evening of April 5, 1970, CHP Unit 78-12 was driven by Officer James Pence with Officer George Alleyn as the passenger officer. Both officers were in full uniform in a marked CHP cruiser.

Officer Alleyn was the senior officer, having joined the CHP in 1967. He was nicknamed "Mike." He grew up in Brownsville, Texas; in 1960, his family moved to the Bay Area of California. He attended high school in Campbell, California, located south of San Jose. After his high school graduation, he enrolled in junior college. For a brief time, he worked as a technician. After his wife Shirley gave birth to their first child, Julie, he applied to the CHP. He turned twenty-four on March 1, 1970, when his second child, Kevin, was nine months old.

Officer Pence was born in Chicago, Illinois, on May 18, 1945. He was nicknamed "Skip." At the age of twenty-four, he was the oldest of the four CHP officers who died in "The Newhall Incident." He attended Armijo High School in Fairfield, California, with his future wife, Janet; they married after their high school graduation. He worked as a welder at the Mare Island Naval Shipyards before applying to the CHP. He reported to the CHP Academy in January 1969 and was assigned to the Newhall Station on May 23, 1969. He and his family lived in a mobile home in Saugus. At the time of death, he had a daughter, Theresa, three, and a son, Jay, fourteen months old.

THE SUSPECTS
Bobby Augusta Davis

The youngest of three children of Floyd and Ellie Davis, Bobby Augusta Davis was born on October 6, 1941, in Ryan, Oklahoma, where he grew up. He dropped out of high school and joined the Marines at eighteen in 1960. He shot and killed another Marine while on guard duty, but the killing was deemed to be an excusable homicide, and he was never charged with a crime or malfeasance of duty in connection with the shooting. However, he received a bad conduct discharge from the Marines in 1962 after he was convicted of a violation of the Dyer Act for driving a stolen car across state lines.

Two years later, Bobby Davis was convicted of bank robbery and sentenced to federal prison. In 1965, he was convicted of assaulting a federal officer and attempting escape while in custody. He was identified in robberies that had been committed before his 1964 bank robbery conviction. In 1968, while still in custody, he was convicted of three counts of armed robbery and three counts of kidnapping committed in 1963 and 1964.

Bobby Davis met and befriended Jack Twining while they were both serving time in Leavenworth Federal Prison.

Davis was paroled in July 1969.

Jack Wright Twining

Born in North Carolina in 1935, Twining claimed that he was an orphan and did not know of any family members.

He was first arrested for burglary in Butler, Pennsylvania, in 1950, when he was fifteen years old. In succeeding years, he was repeatedly arrested for various offenses including larceny, transporting a stolen car across state lines, assaulting a police officer, and bank robbery. He was in almost continuous custody and reputedly spent time in eight of the nine major federal penitentiaries. While in Alcatraz, he killed another inmate in a fight; this homicide was ruled to be in self-defense. Twining was not criminally charged in this incident.

While in Leavenworth Federal Prison, he met and befriended Bobby Davis. He apparently was the "protector" of the slightly built Davis while they were both at Leavenworth. They agreed to meet after they both were released from prison.

Jack Twining was released on parole from federal prison in late April 1969. He absconded from parole shortly after his release; he was wanted as a parole violator in early April 1970.

After his release from prison, Twining committed a robbery of a savings and loan in Decatur, Illinois. He shot and killed the teller when there wasn't enough cash. He was never apprehended or prosecuted for this crime.

Twining and Davis After Release from Prison

As they had agreed, Jack Twining and Bobby Davis reunited after they were paroled. They decided to go to California to commit robberies there.

Bobby Davis obtained a California driver's license under the name of Russell Lowell Talbert, III, by using a license Jack Twining had stolen in Winston-Salem, North Carolina. They purchased a 1964 red Pontiac which they registered under the name of Russell Lowell Talbert, III.

After Davis and Twining arrived in Los Angeles, they rented an apartment on Ximino Street in Long Beach. They had accumulated an arsenal of weapons, including seven handguns, an automatic rifle, and a sawed-off shotgun. They did not keep these weapons in the apartment for fear the apartment manager or a cleaning lady might discover them. Instead, they kept the weapons in the 1964 Pontiac.

After "The Newhall Incident," Sheriff's investigators obtained a search warrant for the Ximino Street apartment. There they found names, addresses, and maps indicating that Twining and Davis were intending to kidnap bank executives and hold them in exchange for ransom.

THE SHOOTOUT

When serviceman Jack Tidwell and his wife had previously observed the 1964 red Pontiac, there was only one occupant in the vehicle. That was Bobby Davis, who had brandished a gun at the Tidwells. Approximately forty minutes later, when the 1964 Pontiac was stopped in the driveway entrance for the Standard Oil station and J's Restaurant, it contained two occupants–Bobby Davis and Jack Twining.

When the Tidwells first encountered the 1964 Pontiac, Bobby Davis and Jack Twining were testing the broadcasting distance of walkie-talkies to use in connection with some bank robberies and possible kidnappings of bank executives they were planning to commit. At that time, Bobby Davis was the sole occupant of the vehicle, but Twining entered the vehicle shortly after Davis' encounter with the Tidwells.

What follows is a step-by-step account of what occurred when Officers Frago and Gore, in Unit 78-8, pulled up behind the 1964 Pontiac, which was stopped in the business access driveway to the Standard Oil station.

1. Officer Gore, the driver of Unit 78-8, and Officer Frago, the passenger, both exited the CHP cruiser.

2. Officer Gore ordered Bobby Davis, the driver of the 1964 Pontiac, to exit and place his hands on the vehicle. Davis got out of the car while Jack Twining remained seated on the passenger side.

3. Officer Gore approached Davis on the driver's side in order to frisk him. Officer Frago, holding a shotgun in port-arms position [the rifle is held diagonally in front of the body with the muzzle pointing upward to the left], walked toward the suspect on the passenger side.

4. The passenger side door suddenly swung open, Twining jumped out, fired two shots into the chest of Officer Frago killing him instantly.

5. Twining fired two shots at Officer Gore that missed. Officer Gore fired a shot at Twining that missed.

6. While Officer Gore was focused on Twining, Davis produced a gun and shot Officer Gore twice in the chest at close range. Officer Gore died instantly.

7. Unit 78-12, containing Officers Pence and Alleyn, arrived and stopped next to Unit 78-8 and behind the 1964 Pontiac. Davis retrieved a 12-guage shotgun from the Pontiac and fired at Unit 78-12. Twining fired at Unit 78-12 with his handgun.

8. After making an "officer needs help" call, Officer Pence exited Unit 78-12, took cover behind the driver's side door, and fired at Davis with his handgun. Officer Alleyn exited on the passenger side of Unit 78-12, ran behind Unit 78-8, took cover behind the passenger door of Unit 78-8, and fired his shotgun at Twining.

9. Officer Alleyn emptied his shotgun and moved to the rear of Unit 78-8 where he was fatally shot by Davis. In the meantime, Twining moved to the driver's side of the Pontiac, giving him a direct line of fire at Officer Pence.

10. Officer Pence emptied his revolver and moved to the rear of Unit 78-12 to reload. As Officer Pence was attempting to reload, Twining shot him four times with his handgun.

11. Twining ran up to the badly wounded Officer Pence, leaned over the fender of Unit 78-12, and shot Officer Pence in the head, killing him instantly. As he fired this shot, Twining was heard to say, "I've got you now, you son of a bitch."

12. Citizen Gary Kness ran to the rear of Unit 78-8 and attempted to drag the prone Officer Alleyn from the line of fire. Kness took Officer Alleyn's gun and fired at Davis, wounding him.

13. Twining and Davis both ran to the 1964 Pontiac and entered it, Twining on the driver's side and Davis on the passenger side.

14. Unit 78-16R, containing Officers Edwin Holmes and Richard Robinson, arrived. They fired at the 1964 Pontiac containing Twining and Davis as it was driving away from the location. Citizen Kness dove into a nearby ditch to avoid the shots fired from the arriving Unit 78-16R.

15. Unit 78-16R took off in pursuit of the 1964 Pontiac. Approximately two miles from the shootout, gunfire from Unit 78-16R disabled the Pontiac. Davis and Twining ran from the vehicle, split up, and vanished in the countryside that bordered both sides of the Golden State Freeway (Interstate 5).

ARREST OF BOBBY DAVIS

On the early morning of April 6, 1970, forty-year-old Dan Schwarz was sleeping alone in his camper that was mounted on a pickup truck. He was parked in an isolated glen beside San Francisquito Canyon Road, northeast of the Golden State Freeway. Schwarz was a tool grinder from Chicago. A seasoned traveler used to traveling alone, he was on vacation.

At about 3:30 a.m., he was awakened by someone attempting to enter his camper. It was Bobby Davis, who shouted, "Let me in." When Schwarz refused, Davis fired a shot into the camper that just missed Schwarz. Davis then threatened to set the camper on fire if Schwarz did not come out.

Schwarz grabbed the .38 revolver he kept inside the camper, opened the door, and jumped out to face the intruder. As the tool grinder and Bobby Davis came face to face outside the camper, they opened fire simultaneously. Davis missed but sustained a gunshot wound to his chest. Wounded and with his gun empty, Davis charged Schwarz, a stocky man, and beat him about the head with his handgun, knocking him semiconscious. Then he grabbed the keys, jumped into the truck and drove off.

Schwarz struggled to his feet and managed to walk to a power station down the road. At about 4:00 a.m., he reported the incident by telephone to the Sheriff's office in Newhall.

A short time later, acting on the information supplied by Dan Schwarz, Sheriff's Deputies Fred Thatcher and Don Yates spotted the stolen pick-up with camper on top about three miles down a dirt road extension of San Francisquito Canyon Road. They stopped Davis and ordered him out of the truck. He surrendered without a struggle.

At the time of his arrest, Davis was identified as Russell Lowell Talbert, III, based on the registration and stolen identification found in the Pontiac. Davis refused to make any statements. Since he was injured, he was taken to the Golden State Hospital in Newhall, where he was treated for his wounds. Later, he was transferred to the prison ward of the Los Angeles County-USC Medical Center to await arraignment in the Newhall Municipal Court on murder charges.

THE SUICIDE OF JACK TWINING

Bobby Davis had traveled northbound after he and Jack Twining had split up after the shootout. Twining traveled south.

Steven and Betty Hoag and their seventeen-year-old son lived in a large ranch-style home on Pico Canyon Road in Stevenson Ranch. On the morning of April 6, 1970, at 4:30 a.m., Steven was awake and preparing to go to work as a cement truck driver. Betty was also up preparing breakfast for Steven before he left for work.

Steven Hoag had gone outside and was confronted by Jack Twining, who was holding a shotgun. The shotgun was the weapon that had been held by Officer Frago when he was shot by Twining. From inside the house, Betty Hoag observed Twining holding a handgun and pointing the shotgun at her husband. She quickly ran to the telephone and called the Highway Patrol office, located less than a block away. Just as she finished the call, her husband and Twining entered the house. Twining stated that as long as everyone did what he said, he wasn't going to hurt anyone. He proceeded to eat the trucker's breakfast of eggs and toast. Twining told the Hoags that he had been in trouble most of his life and this was probably the end of the line for him; he had just killed three cops near Castaic.

During Twining's recitation, there was a knock at the door. Thinking it was her son who slept in a cottage next to the house, Betty Hoag answered the door. It was a highway patrolman. He grabbed Mrs. Hoag, pulled her out of the house and led her away to safety. Awakened by the commotion around the house, the Hoags' seventeen-year-old son also slipped away to safety.

Steven Hoag was now alone in the house with Jack Twining while over 200 Sheriff's deputies and highway patrol officers surrounded the house, along with helicopters hovering overhead. Lieutenant Oliver Taylor of the Sheriff's Office called the Hoag residence, spoke to Twining, and urged him to release his hostage and surrender. Twining even talked to a newsman who phoned the house. One of the calls involved a conversation between Jack Twining and Sergeant John Brady of the Los Angeles County Sheriff's Office, as follows:

SGT. BRADY: *This is Sergeant Brady of the L.A. Sheriff's Office. How is everything in there?*

TWINING: *Fine, everything's just fine. We're just sitting here watching the sun come up.*

SGT. BRADY: *Why don't you come on out and we'll talk about this?*

TWINING: *Nope! I'll stay here.*

SGT. BRADY: *What about Mr. Hoag? Can he come out?*

TWINING: *Nope! He'll stay, too, 'til I decide what to do.*

SGT. BRADY: *Come on, there are at least a hundred officers out here. You aren't going to get away. There's no sense in getting somebody hurt.*

TWINING: *Nobody will get hurt unless one of those hundred officers does something stupid!*

SGT. BRADY: *What happened earlier tonight?*

TWINING: *Well, I don't rightly know. They stopped us. We were ready; they weren't. One of them got real careless, so I wasted him. Did you get my partner?*

SGT. BRADY: *Talbert?*

TWINING: *Uh, yeah.*

SGT. BRADY: *They picked him up a few minutes ago. He gave up.*

TWINING: *I want to talk to him.*

SGT. BRADY: *Come on out, and we'll let you do that.*

TWINING: *Naw, you bring him here.*

SGT. BRADY: *I can't, he got hurt. He's in the hospital.*

TWINING: *Get him on the phone.*

SGT. BRADY: *What?*

TWINING: *Goddammit! I said get him on the phone! Get me his number so I can call or have him call me!*

(End of conversation.)

Jack Twining then had the following conversation with Bobby Davis:

SCOVAL: *This is Deputy Scoval calling from the jail ward of the USC Medical Center. Hold on, please.*

DAVIS: *Hello, Jack.*

TWINING: *Talbert?*

DAVIS: *Yeah.*

TWINING: *How are you? Are you hurt?*

DAVIS: *Not too good, my throat hurts. I got hit in the chest.*

TWINING: *Did you get it in the shootout?*

DAVIS:	*No – later.*
TWINING:	*I'm thinking of popping it off.*
DAVIS:	*I don't blame you, Jack. I wish I'd gotten one in the head myself.*
TWINING:	*I'm just trying to make up my mind to do it. All I need is time to get up my nerve. Then I'm going to pop it off.*
DAVIS:	*I guess that might be the best thing to do.*
TWINING:	*Well, you don't sound too good. I'll let you go.*
DAVIS:	*Okay, Jack.*
TWINING:	*I don't want to go back to jail. As soon as I work up to it, I'm going to blow the top of my head off.*
DAVIS:	*Jack, I wish you wouldn't.*
TWINING:	*I'll see you, buddy.*

Finally, shortly after 9:00 a.m., Jack Twining gave Steven Hoag a $100 bill and told deputies that he was releasing his prisoner. Hoag walked away from the residence, leaving Twining alone inside. Lieutenant Taylor called Twining and told him that he had until 10:00 to come out or they would come in and get him.

At 10:00 a.m., with no response from Twining inside the house, officers fired a series of tear gas rounds into the house. Five officers wearing flak jackets, helmets, and gas masks rushed into the house. Just after they entered, they heard a shotgun blast fired by Twining. They returned fire, but it was not necessary. Twining had committed suicide by putting the muzzle of the shotgun taken from Officer Frago beneath his chin and pulling the trigger. The force of the shotgun blast had shattered his head.

Jack Twining was dead. Bobby Davis was in custody. Their reign of terror, lasting over ten hours, was over.

THE TRIAL

On April 6, 1970, Deputy District Attorney James M. Ideman received a call to come downtown to see Chief Deputy District Attorney Joseph Busch. As Chief Deputy, Busch was responsible for overseeing the day-to-day operations of the District Attorney's Office. Busch told Ideman that he wanted him to handle the case involving the murders of the four CHP officers. He stated this was a case the office had to win, and that Ideman was authorized to do whatever was needed to successfully prosecute the case.

James Ideman charged Bobby Augusta Davis with four counts of first-degree murder, one count for each of the four dead officers. The prosecution was seeking the death penalty. Within a month after his arrest, Davis was bound over for trial after a preliminary hearing before Judge Adrian Adams of the Newhall Municipal Court. The case was assigned to the courtroom of Superior Court Judge L. Thaxton Hanson for trial.

Judge Lloyd Thaxton Hanson

L. Thaxton Hanson was a trial judge whose rulings tended to favor the prosecution. He was born in 1920 and served in the United States Army in both World War II and the Korean War. He was admitted to the California State Bar in July 1954; he was a lawyer in private practice from 1954 to 1968.

In August 1968, California Governor Ronald Reagan appointed Hanson as a judge in the Los Angeles Superior Court. He served in that capacity until July 24, 1973, when Reagan appointed him as an associate justice in the California Court of Appeal, where he served from July 25, 1973, until his retirement on May 1, 1990. He died on September 30, 1993.

Prosecutor James M. Ideman

James M. Ideman, the lead prosecutor in the case against Bobby Augusta Davis, had a remarkable career; both as a prosecutor and as a state and federal judge.

He was born on April 2, 1931, in Rockford, Illinois. He had a strong military background: he attended high school at the Riverside Military Academy in Gainesville, Georgia, graduated from The Citadel in 1953, and served in the United States Army, Special Services, 82nd Airborne Division, from 1953 to 1956, achieving the rank of First Lieutenant. From 1965 to 1984, he served as a military judge hearing courts martial on active reserve.

Mr. Ideman graduated from the University of Southern California Law Center in 1963 and was hired as a deputy district attorney for the County of Los Angeles on January 2, 1964. He was an excellent trial lawyer who prosecuted many serious cases. He obtained five death penalty verdicts and also convicted brothers Paul and Tom Ferguson for the 1968 murder of silent film screen actor Ramon Novarro.

James Ideman ran in the November 1978 election for an open seat on the Los Angeles Superior Court. He won, becoming the first prosecutor elected (rather than appointed) to the Los Angeles Superior Court. He resigned his position as a deputy district attorney and was sworn in as a judge on January 8, 1979.

On May 24, 1984, President Ronald Reagan nominated him to the federal bench, and he was confirmed by the U. S. Senate on June 15, 1984. Ideman served as a U. S. District Court judge until he retired in Septem-

ber 1998. After his retirement, he sat as an assigned judge on the Los Angeles Superior Court until his final retirement in 2006. His career included
fifteen years as a prosecutor and twenty-seven years as a judge on both
state and federal courts.

ADDITIONAL INVESTIGATION

The prosecution was seeking the death penalty against Bobby Augusta
Davis. The murder of four CHP officers would seem sufficient by itself to
justify the death penalty, but prosecutor Ideman wanted to investigate
Davis' background to determine if additional evidence could be uncov-
ered to use at a penalty phase. In the summer of 1970, Ideman and lead
investigator Sergeant John Brady visited various locations in the United
States where Davis had committed crimes or served time. Their travels included a trip to Atlanta, Georgia, where a former crime partner of Davis,
named Jim Travis Ward, was on parole. Ward was interviewed by Ideman
and Sgt. Brady and told them of a murder committed in 1963 by him and
Davis during a residential robbery. Ideman and Brady returned to Los
Angeles with powerful additional evidence to use at a penalty phase.

THE GUILT PHASE

Below is an overview of the primary individuals and charges,
and the history of the guilt phase of the case against Bobby Augusta Davis.

PEOPLE V. BOBBY AUGUSTA DAVIS
Case B112487

JUDGE: The Honorable L. Thaxton Hanson
PROSECUTORS: James M. Ideman, Deputy District Attorney

DEFENSE ATTORNEYS:	Sterling E. Norris, Deputy District Attorney Marvin Schwartz, Deputy Public Defender Richard Plotin, Deputy Public Defender Four
CHARGES:	counts of first-degree murder
COURTROOM:	Los Angeles Superior Court Van Nuys Courthouse, Department F

IMPORTANT DATES: May 26, 1970: October 7, 1970: November 12, 1970: November 13, 1970:	Defendant arraigned; pleads not guilty Guilt phase of jury trial begins Closing arguments; jury instructed; jury re- tires to deliberate Jury convicts defendant of four counts of first-degree murder

THE PENALTY PHASE

After Bobby Augusta Davis was convicted of first-degree murder, the same jury was to determine whether he should receive the death penalty or serve a sentence of life in prison. To assist the jury in making this determination, the case included a penalty phase in which the prosecution and the defense could introduce evidence on the convicted defendant's background and history. Normally during this phase, the prosecution would introduce evidence of the defendant's criminal history and violent acts; the defense would try to mitigate or minimize the defendant's role in the crime and introduce evidence of a dysfunctional and abusive childhood.

Prosecutor James Ideman had a wealth of ammunition for the penalty phase. First, he argued the horrific nature of the crimes alone for which Davis was convicted warranted the imposition of the ultimate penalty.

Four young peace officers had lost their lives based on the brutal and cold-blooded acts of Bobby Davis. Second, Ideman introduced the prior crimes for which Davis had been convicted. These included convictions for assaulting a federal officer, attempted escape, multiple robberies and multiple kidnappings.

If that weren't enough, prosecutor Ideman had a bombshell for the jury: he called Jim Travis Ward, the former crime partner of Bobby Davis. Ward testified that sometime in 1963, he and Davis had followed a waitress (a Mrs. Barrett) from a closing diner to her home in hopes of robbing her of the daily receipts. Mrs. Barrett lived at home with her husband and daughter. Davis and Ward broke into the house and, in full view of the Barretts' thirteen-year-old daughter, Judy, Davis shot and killed Mr. Barrett with a .32 automatic pistol. Under California law, the testimony of an accomplice is not admissible as evidence unless it is corroborated by independent evidence. The next witness called by Ideman was Judy Barrett LaBella, the daughter: Ideman hoped her testimony would furnish the required corroboration. Although she was unable to identify the defendant in the courtroom, evidence was introduced that when previously shown a photograph of Bobby Davis, she became very emotional and distraught. A psychiatrist testified that her reaction to Davis' photograph was the result of the repressed memory of a traumatic event. Judge Hanson ruled this furnished sufficient corroboration of Ward's testimony, enabling the jury to consider this evidence of another murder that had been committed by Bobby Davis.

On November 23, 1970, the jury returned a verdict of death for each of the four counts of first-degree murder for which the defendant had been convicted.

On November 25, 1970, Judge Hanson denied defense motions for a new trial and for reduction of the penalty and sentenced Bobby Augusta Davis to die in California's gas chamber for each of the four counts of which he was convicted. Judge Hanson also ordered Davis to be transported by the Sheriff of Los Angeles County to San Quentin prison for imposition of the sentence.

THE APPEAL

On February 17, 1972, while Davis' appeal was pending, the California Supreme Court issued its opinion in *People v. Anderson*, 6 Cal.3d 628 (1972). In a 4-3 decision, the Court ruled that California's death penalty statute was unconstitutional since it provided for "cruel and unusual punishment."

There were 107 persons on California's death row at the time of the *Anderson* decision, and their death sentences were reduced to life imprisonment with the possibility of parole. California's murder statute had provided for a sentence of either the death penalty or life imprisonment with the possibility of parole upon a conviction of first-degree murder. With the death penalty having been declared unconstitutional in California, all the death penalties reverted to the alternative penalty – life imprisonment with the possibility of parole.

Among the persons on California's death row who benefited from the *Anderson* decision were Charles Manson and five members of his family, Sirhan Sirhan, "Onion Field" killer Gregory Powell, and Bobby Augusta Davis.

EPILOGUE

The 107 persons on death row whose death sentences were reduced to life imprisonment represented the worst of the criminals in California's prison system. These 107 inmates were now entitled to parole hearings to determine their suitability for release on parole. Some of them were actually released on parole.

Bobby Augusta Davis had approximately twelve parole hearings, but he was always found unsuitable for release. The horrific nature of the crimes for which he was convicted was undoubtedly the primary reason he was denied parole; his psychological profile also indicated he would be a danger to society if released.

Both Jack Twining and Bobby Davis died by committing suicide. As stated earlier, Jack Twining committed suicide a few hours after his involvement in the murder of the four young CHP officers. Bobby Davis took his own life over thirty-nine years later. On August 16, 2009, Bobby Augusta Davis was found dead from hanging in his cell at Kern Valley State Prison. He was sixty-seven-years-old.

LESSONS LEARNED

"The Newhall Incident" was one of the most analyzed shootings in the history of law enforcement. This analysis has included: the training of cadets at the CHP Academy, the weaponry used by officers, the CHP's emphasis on courtesy and lack of confrontation during vehicle stops rather than officer safety, the lack of experienced training officers to work with newly assigned officers, and even the dress code. However, such a broad analysis is beyond the scope of this chapter since any deficiencies in these areas have been corrected in the many years since "The Newhall Incident." Instead, this section will discuss tactical errors made by the victim officers.

The four CHP officers who died in "The Newhall Incident" were working two-man vehicles. The CHP began using two-man vehicles for the graveyard shift in 1960 after Officer Richard D. Duvall was shot and murdered during a traffic stop by an escaped convict who had committed an armed robbery. The purpose of the two-man vehicle policy was to enhance officer safety during the nighttime hours. However, the maximum benefit of two-man police vehicles can only be achieved by proper coordination and tactics between the two officers.

Officers Gore and Frago were lifelong friends who joined the CHP at the same time. They were partners on patrol the entire time they spent with the CHP. Neither officer had worked on patrol with an experienced training officer. The current practice is for a two-man police vehicle to include one experienced training officer with a rookie officer, or to have two well-trained officers working together.

In "The Newhall Incident," the initial police call referred to a man brandishing a gun from a clearly described vehicle. Officers Gore and Frago were, therefore, aware there was a gun inside the car. At the time, CHP policy for such a "hot stop" was for the driver-officer to be the "contact officer" and approach the driver of the car. The passenger-officer would be the "cover officer," remaining behind the CHP vehicle in a covering position.

Initially, Officers Gore and Frago deployed in this manner with Gore approaching Bobby Davis, the driver of the vehicle, and Frago taking a cover position by the front of the police cruiser. There were several commands by the officers for the occupants to exit the vehicle with their hands up. Davis eventually exited the vehicle, and Officer Gore began to search him. In the meantime, Jack Twining remained seated on the passenger side. Officer Frago had a shotgun and initially maintained a cover position at the rear of the suspects' vehicle, but he abandoned this position by walking to the passenger side of the vehicle, apparently to order Twining out of the car. As Officer Frago reached the passenger door, it suddenly swung open, and Twining fired two rounds in Officer Frago's chest, killing him instantly. Twining quickly exited the car and fired two shots at Officer Gore, which missed. Officer Gore, who had holstered his revolver while searching Davis, drew his service revolver and fired a shot at Twining, which missed. While Officer Gore was occupied with Twining, Davis produced a gun from his waistband and fired two shots into Officer Gore's chest, killing him instantly.

Officers Gore and Frago had approached the red Pontiac containing Davis and Twining before their backup unit arrived. By proceeding prematurely, they forfeited the tactical advantage that a second two-man police unit would have provided. Officers Pence and Alleyn arrived at the scene just as Officer Gore fell to the ground, fatally wounded. In the subsequent shootout with Davis and Twining, both Officer Pence and Officer Alleyn were shot and killed.

More than four decades later, nearly all police officers know about "The Newhall Incident." This tragedy, like "The Onion Field" incident seven years earlier, resulted in major improvements to tactical training across the country.

- Positioning to maintain cover and concealment while giving verbal commands to vehicle occupants during dangerous stops is essential.

- Six-shot revolvers are not the weapon of choice in modern times, given the nature of the weapons that officers now face.

- In addition, note that both Officers Gore and Frago were killed by shots to their chests. Wearing body armor (not widely done at the time) may have made an essential difference in the officers' survivability and their ability to return fire and neutralize the threat despite being shot. All uniformed patrol officers ought to wear body armor.

The Newhall Incident

Carswell Wins on
Nomination Test

HERALD EXAMINER

4 CHP OFFICERS SLAIN

One Suspect Kills Self; Nab Second

The Los Angeles Herald-Examiner *and other newspapers, both in and out of California, carried the tragic story on their front pages Monday, April 6, 1970.*

Roger D. Gore

Walter C. Frago

CHP officers Roger Gore and Walt Frago, responding to a report of a motorist brandishing a firearm, stopped a red Pontiac at J's Coffee Shop near present-day Magic Mountain Parkway.
James Pence and George "Mike" Alleyn radioed Gore and Frago that they would roll in behind them as backup.

James E. Pence, Jr.

George M. Alleyn

Walter Carroll Frago

Officer
Walt Frago

- Born:
  - December 22, 1946
- Died:
  - April 5, 1970
- Born and raised in Merced California
  - Attended Merced High School where he became best friends with Roger Gore
- Joined CHP at same time as Roger Gore
  - Both reported to same CHP training class in Sacramento in August, 1968
  - Both assigned to Newhall Station on December 12, 1968
  - Partners
  - Families lived a block apart in Newhall
- Survived by wife Nikki and Daughters Amorette (age 4) and Gabrielle (age 3)

Roger David Gore

Officer
Roger Gore

- Born:
  - February 17, 1947
- Died:
  - April 5, 1970
- Born and raised in Merced, California
  - Attended Merced High School where he became best friends with Walt Frago
- Joined CHP at same time as Walt Frago
  - Both reported to same CHP training class in Sacramento in August, 1968
  - Both assigned to Newhall Station on December 12, 1968
  - Partners
  - Families lived a block apart in Newhall
- Survived by wife Valerie and daughter Elyse (age 18 months)

James Edward Pence, Jr.

Officer
James Pence

- Born:
  - May 18, 1945
- Died:
  - April 5, 1970
- Born in Chicago, Illinois
  - Nicknamed "Skip"
  - Attended Armijo High in Fairfield with future wife Janet
    - Married after they graduated high school
  - Welder at Mare Island Naval Shipyards before applying to C.H.P.
- Reported to C.H.P. Academy in January, 1969
  - Assigned to Newhall Station on May 23, 1969
  - Lived in a mobile home in Saugus
- Survived by wife Janet and daughter Theresa (age 3) and son Jay (age 14 months)

George Michael Alleyn

Officer
George Alleyn

- Born:
  - March 1, 1946
- Died:
  - April 5, 1970
- Grew up in Brownsville, Texas
  - Nicknamed "Mike"
  - Family moved to Bay Area in California in 1960
  - Attended high school in Campbell, California (South of San Jose)
  - Enrolled in Junior College
  - Job as technician for IBM
  - Got married and had a child
- Applied to C.H.P. in 1967
- Survived by wife Shirley, daughter Julie (age 3) and son Kevin (age 9 months)

Bobby Augusta Davis Booking Photo April 6, 1970

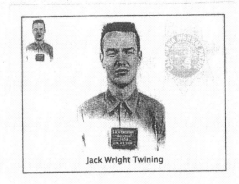

Jack Wright Twining

- **Born:**
  - November 13, 1942 in Ponca City, Oklahoma
- **Early Childhood:**
  - Ponca City, Oklahoma
- **Military Career:**
  - Joined Marines in 1960
    - Killed another soldier while on guard duty
    - Received bad conduct discharge in 1962 after Dyer Act conviction

- Age 34 on April 5, 1970
- **Criminal History:**
  - Spent time in eight of the nine major federal penitentiaries
    - In custody almost continuously since age 16
    - Met and befriended Bobby Augusta Davis in Leavenworth
    - At Alcatraz, killed another inmate in a fight (ruled self-defense)
    - Released from federal prison in late April, 1969
    - Absconded from parole shortly after release
  - Committed a robbery of a Savings & Loan in Decatur, Illinois
    - Shot and killed victim when there wasn't enough cash

- **Early Criminal History:**
  - Convicted in 1964 of bank robbery and sentenced to federal prison
  - Convicted in 1965 of assaulting a federal officer and attempted escape while in custody
  - Convicted in 1968 of armed robbery (3 counts) and kidnapping (3 counts) committed in 1963 and 1964
  - Paroled in July, 1969
- **Miscellaneous:**
  - Met and befriended Jack Twining while they were in Leavenworth Federal Prison

37

The two CHP vehicles containing the victim officers

October 14, 1970 widows of CHP shooting victims wait in D.A.'s library before entering Van Nuys Court. Left to right: Mrs. Roger D. Gore, Mrs. Walter C. Frago, Mrs. George M. Alleyn, Mrs. James E. Pence.

Gary Kness receiving a community service award from the CHP for coming to the assistance of the four Newhall officers and exchanging gunfire with the killers

Former Deputy District Attorney James Ideman (left), District Attorney Steve Cooley and California Highway Patrol Commissioner Joseph Farrow at a ceremony in which a stretch of Interstate 5 was dedicated to honor the four CHP Officers who were killed in the line of duty

Memorial for the four officers at Newhall CHP Station

CHAPTER TWO

Detective Arleigh McCree and
Officer Ronald Ball
Los Angeles Police Department
"This Bomb is Booby Trapped"

February 8, 1986

DETECTIVE ARLEIGH McCREE

AT THE TIME OF HIS DEATH, on February 8, 1986, Arleigh McCree had achieved legendary status within the Los Angeles Police Department. He was considered one of the world's leading experts on explosives and international terrorism.

McCree was born on December 24, 1939, in Bush, Illinois, and grew up in Kentucky. His father worked as a blaster in the coal mines of Kentucky, and young Arleigh learned about explosives from him. McCree later served in the United States Navy and greatly increased his knowledge of explosives as a diver handling underwater demolition assignments.

He joined the Los Angeles Police Department in 1965. In 1979, he became the Officer in Charge of the Firearms and Explosives Unit.

In 1983, he went to Lebanon to help investigate the bombing of the U. S. Marine Corps barracks. In 1984, he played a major role in coordinating security for the Olympic Games in Los Angeles.

Los Angeles Police Department officials confirmed that in 1981, Libyan dictator Muammar Gaddafi offered McCree $140,000 to train terrorists. "They wanted me to be the leader and recruit the rest of my guys," McCree was quoted as saying.

McCree enjoyed SCUBA diving during his off-duty time. He was survived by his wife, Edith, and a son and a daughter from a previous marriage.

OFFICER RONALD BALL

Ronald Ball was born on December 12, 1942. He joined the Los Angeles Police Department in 1970. In his career, he worked out of the LAPD's Van Nuys Division as a patrol officer. He joined the Firearms and Explosives Unit in 1980 and was considered an expert bomb technician.

Ball was an outdoorsman who liked to fish and occasionally went to Placerita Canyon to fish. At the time of his death, he had been a member of the bomb squad for about six years and was planning to retire in three years.

He was survived by his wife of nearly twenty-five years, Ann Ball, two teenage daughters, Stacy and Tiffany, and a young son.

DONALD LEE MORSE

Donald Lee Morse was born on August 21, 1949, in Sanford, Florida. He was the third of ten children in an African-American family that included six sisters and three brothers. He grew up in an intact family home and worked in the family's grocery business and later in his father's construction business. In 1967, he graduated from Lyman High School in Longwood, Florida.

Morse attended beauty school in Orlando, Florida, graduating in 1969. From 1970 to 1973, he and a partner operated a beauty salon. Morse wanted to learn how to do makeup, and he obtained a job on a movie being filmed in New Mexico. In 1976, he moved to Burbank, California when NBC offered him a permanent job as a makeup artist. During this time, he worked for Columbia Pictures as a makeup artist.

Morse was a member of the Makeup Artists and Hairstylists Union, Local 706. He was very critical of the way the union was being run by Howard Smit, the union's business representative. On January 16, 1986, Morse came to the union office after 6:00 p.m. to pay his dues. He told a secretary that he did not like the way the place was being run. He was told to go to an executive board meeting. He asked the secretary whether Howard [Smit] was there; he was told that Howard was gone. He stated, "That's okay. I know how to deal with them. I've got something for them." He then left and slammed the door.

SHOOTING OF HOWARD SMIT

On February 4, 1986, shortly after 11:00 p.m., Howard Smit and three other persons were leaving an executive board meeting at the union offices on Chandler Boulevard in Van Nuys. They were in the rear parking lot when five or six shots were fired in their direction from behind a nearby fence. One of the shots struck Howard Smit, entering the left side of his chest traveling across his ribs and exiting on the right side of his chest. No one else was struck by the gunfire. Victim Smit was taken to the hospital for medical treatment and survived his injuries.

One of the persons in the parking lot told the police that he looked in the direction of the shots and "observed a male Negro with a knit cap." However, he was unable to make a further identification.

Five slugs were recovered from the crime scene. One slug was analyzed as a spent bullet, .38 or .357 magnum caliber.

Police investigators believed that Donald Morse may have been involved in the shooting because of the threatening remarks he had made on January 16, 1986. He fit the general description of the suspect since he was a male African-American. Also, on May 18, 1984, Morse had been arrested for rape, and a .38 caliber revolver was observed in his residence at 6849 Vanscoy Avenue, North Hollywood. However, the gun was not booked and remained in Morse's possession.[1]

SERVICE OF SEARCH WARRANT

On February 8, 1986, at approximately 7:30 a.m., police officers from the Los Angeles Police Department served a search warrant at the home of Donald Morse at 6849 Vanscoy Avenue, North Hollywood, to look for the gun used in the shooting of Howard Smit. Donald Morse was in his bedroom at the residence when the warrant was served. Also living at the lo-

---

[1] *Although he was a suspect in the Smit shooting, Morse was never directly connected to the crime, and he was never charged in the incident.*

cation in different bedrooms were his brother, Alvin Morse, and his sister, Ernestine, and her three children.

Officers first searched the main residence. On the top shelf of Donald Morse's bedroom closet, they found a box wrapped with tape. Inside the box were shotgun shells wrapped in tape and some .22 caliber and .38 caliber rounds.

The officers wanted to search the garage, but it was locked. Morse was asked for the keys. He gave them to an officer. Officer Asvonanda went to the garage with the keys, unlocked the garage door, and began a search. He opened a cabinet in the center of the garage. From a shelf, he removed a metal pipe three to four inches in diameter, nine inches long, capped at both ends, with wires and an attached battery. The wires led from the pipe back into the cabinet. Officer Asvonanda carefully placed the pipe on the floor of the garage. He left the garage and told Detective Harley, who was in charge of the investigation, what he had found in the garage.

Detective Harley entered the garage and observed that the wires were connected to a second larger pipe on the shelf in the cabinet. Morse was brought to the garage. Detective Harley questioned him about what appeared to be an explosive device in his garage. Morse replied that he had never seen it before and further stated that he let a man and a woman store their property in the garage.

Morse was placed under arrest and transported to the police station. The house was evacuated, and the Los Angeles Police Department's bomb squad was notified.

DEATHS OF DETECTIVE ARLEIGH McCREE AND OFFICER RONALD BALL

February 8, 1986 was a Saturday, and Arleigh McCree was at home on a day off. He was notified of the discovery of the two pipe bombs in the garage at the residence in North Hollywood. As the officer-in-charge of the bomb squad, he could have allowed other officers in his unit to handle the call. Instead, he personally went to the North Hollywood residence. Detective McCree and Officer Ronald Ball arrived at 6849 Vanscoy Avenue, North Hollywood, later in the morning.

Officer Ball took photographs of both pipe bombs; they then dismantled the smaller bomb. Officer Ball took a small portion of the powder that had been removed from the dismantled pipe bomb, went outside the garage and lit a match to the powder which rapidly burned.

Officer Ball and Detective Douglass of the Criminal Conspiracy Section were inside the garage when Detective McCree began to disarm the second pipe bomb. McCree stated, "It's booby trapped, get out of here," to Detective Douglass, who left the garage and closed the door behind him. Officer Ball was standing behind Detective McCree, who continued his attempts to disarm the pipe bomb. Ten or fifteen seconds later, the pipe bomb exploded. Detective Douglass was standing outside the garage and heard "a deafening noise" and "felt a blast pressure wave." He forced open the side door of the garage and entered. He observed the inside of the garage to be badly damaged with several fires burning. The bodies of Detective McCree and Officer Ball were lying on the garage floor. They had sustained massive injuries. McCree was killed instantly by the blast, and Ball was pronounced dead about an hour later at the Medical Center of North Hollywood.

Deputy Medical Examiner Susan Selser of the Los Angeles County Coroner's Office performed the autopsies on both officers. On February 10, 1986, Dr. Selser ascribed the cause of Detective McCree's death to "multiple injuries." Dr. Selser began counting and identifying each shrapnel wound and stopped counting when she reached wound number 115. Officer McCree's right lower leg and foot had almost been severed, and there was near amputation of his left hand. There was a skull fracture and a gaping laceration severing most of the left side of the neck.

Dr. Selser performed the autopsy of Officer Ronald Ball on February 11, 1986. She ascribed the cause of death to "multiple injuries." The injuries included multiple abrasions, contusions, and puncture lacerations to the body; amputation of the left and right hands at the wrist; extensive trauma to the right leg with near amputation; puncture of the right eye; shrapnel that penetrated the brain; and multiple skull fractures.

DESCRIPTION OF THE BOMBS

After the explosion, Detective David Weller, second in command to Arleigh McCree at the Bomb Unit, arrived at the scene and took charge of the investigation. He observed Officer Ball's camera in the rubble in the garage, retrieved it, and had the film developed. The photographs provided a clear visual of the pipe bombs.

Detective Weller described the bombs as comprising a master bomb that was twelve inches long and a secondary, or slave bomb, that was nine inches long. Inside each bomb were four 12-gauge Remington Peters number six-shot cartridges that were taped together. Pyrodex, a low-grade explosive similar to black powder, filled the pipe cavity. A light bulb filament led from the Pyrodex through a drilled hole to two nine-volt batteries taped to the outside of the master bomb. Wires connected the batteries to the triggering mechanism, which was a wood block containing a folded piece of metal and a soldered wire. Black nylon fishing line was tied to the triggering mechanism, and bungee cords were wrapped around each bomb.

Detective Weller testified in subsequent court proceedings that the bungee cords were designed to attach the bombs to a car. When the car moved, the nylon fishing line would become taut, activating the triggering mechanism resulting in detonation. The bombs were designed to kill people, since they relied upon the movement of human beings to detonate them. The bombs were also designed to fragment and explode shrapnel.

CRIME SCENE INVESTIGATION

Investigators conducted a thorough search of the residence and garage of 6849 Vanscoy, North Hollywood, where Donald Morse resided. Items recovered included:

- A roll of nylon fishing line found in Donald Morse's garage that matched the line used on the bomb's triggering mechanism.

- Morse's van, which was parked in the garage, contained two 9-volt batteries and a bungee cord, both similar to those used on the bombs.

- On a closed cabinet shelf in Morse's kitchen, concealed in a sealed three-pound coffee can, was a container of Pyrodex (the explosive material contained in the pipe bombs).

- "The Anarchist Cookbook," a book about making bombs, was found in the den of Morse's residence. His fingerprints were on the cover of the book and on pages 113-114, beginning the chapter titled "Explosives and Booby Traps."

- Morse's fingerprints, and only his, were found in the three-pound coffee can, the Pyrodex container, the garage cabinet, and on cans in that cabinet.

DETECTIVE JIMMY TRAHIN ACCOUNT

Jimmy Trahin was often my partner on patrol when I was a reserve officer for the LAPD working Newton Division. We became and remain good friends. In April 1977, Officer Trahin was assigned to the Firearms and Explosives Unit where he remained for the next fourteen years until his retirement in August 1991. He gave the following account of the events of February 8, 1986.

Detective Arleigh McCree was the officer-in-charge of the Firearms and Explosives Unit. On Friday afternoon February 7, 1986, Detective McCree held a briefing with the members of the Unit. He had a rotating schedule where two officers from the unit were on call to handle duty call-outs over the weekend. McCree and Officer Ronald Ball would be on call that weekend, and Jimmy Trahin would be the backup with his explosive detection canine, TNT, even though he was scheduled to teach a training class on Saturday. Everyone walked out of the office in anticipation of a slow weekend.

On Saturday, Jimmy Trahin dismissed his class for lunch. His pager went off, and he called Detective Headquarters for messages. A female detective answered, and Trahin identified himself. She started crying and finally composed herself to state that Arleigh and Ron were dead; they were taking a bomb apart in a garage, and it went off. Trahin was needed to get to the crime scene as soon as possible.

Trahin drove home, changed into his Bomb Squad utility uniform, and then drove to the crime scene in North Hollywood. Officer Ron Ball had been taken away in an ambulance, but Detective McCree's body was still in the garage. Trahin entered the garage and observed McCree lying on his back in the middle of the garage. He was barely recognizable with numerous shrapnel wounds on his face, and several of his limbs were barely connected.

During this time, Chief of Police Daryl Gates arrived at the crime scene and spoke to Trahin. He stated that he understood that Trahin was close to Officer Ball. Trahin responded that he and Ron shared common interests and that they frequently socialized. In fact, the two officers and their wives had recently spent a weekend together in Las Vegas. Chief Gates was concerned that the families of the deceased officers would learn about the deaths through the news media. He wanted Trahin to immediately contact Officer Ball's wife, Ann, and tell her what happened. It would be best if the news came from someone she knew and trusted. Trahin agreed. Chief Gates put his hand on Trahin's shoulder and stated, "Just hang on ... we'll get through this together."

A police helicopter took Trahin to Simi Valley where it landed on a high school athletic field. A Simi Valley Police car took him to the vicinity of the Ball residence. Trahin then walked by himself to the front door and rang the doorbell. Ron Ball's teenage daughter, Stacy, answered the door and stated that her father was out on a call. She wondered what Trahin was doing in his uniform. Trahin replied that he wanted to speak to her mother, Ann. Stacy stated that she was at a car wash raising money for their son's local Boy Scout troop in a shopping center parking lot. Trahin asked if she could direct him to the shopping center.

Suddenly Stacy's mood changed, and she asked if something was wrong. She asked if something had happened to her dad. Before Trahin could respond, Stacy realized what was happening and began to cry. All Trahin could say was that he was sorry. They hugged for several minutes, and both cried as Trahin explained briefly what had happened. Trahin told her that it was important that he inform her mother before she heard it from the news media. Trahin and Stacy then went to the Simi Valley Police car and were driven to the shopping center.

The police car parked behind a building out of view. Trahin walked alone across the parking lot. Ann Ball spotted him, ran in his direction, and gave him a kiss on the cheek. She wondered what he was doing there and stated that Ron was out on a call. Trahin stated that he just wanted to talk to her. They walked slowly toward the hidden police car. As they approached the corner of the building, Ann spotted the police car and Stacy standing next to it. Suddenly Ann stopped dead in her tracks and looked directly at Trahin with a horrific look of panic. She grabbed him and stated, "Jimmy, tell me it's not Ron." Trahin could only say, "I'm sorry." She completely broke down, crying and screaming, yelling, "Not my Ron!" They held on to each other and cried together for some time. It was one of the worst experiences of Trahin's life.

The Simi Valley Police car drove up, and Ann and Stacy united in their sorrow. There were a couple of family grief counselors present, and they took over. Trahin said goodbye and returned by helicopter to the crime scene in North Hollywood. Chief Gates was still there. Trahin advised the Chief that the notification had been made, and Chief Gates thanked him.

CRIMINAL CHARGES FILED

On February 12, 1986, the Los Angeles County District Attorney's Office filed a felony complaint against Donald Lee Morse alleging four counts— two counts of murder and two counts involving possession of a destructive device. Morse remained in custody without bail.

Deputy District Attorney Sterling E. "Ernie" Norris of the Special Trials Unit was assigned to prosecute the case. He was hired as a Deputy District Attorney in December 1967 and was assigned to the Van Nuys Branch Office where he spent the following six years prosecuting felony cases. He specialized in the prosecution of murder cases, in which he had a high conviction rate. Homicide detectives admired Norris' work ethic and courtroom skills; they sought him to prosecute their murder cases pending in the Van Nuys Branch Office. In the early 1970s, he prosecuted eight murder cases in one calendar year in which he convicted each defendant of first- or second-degree murder. In 1980, Norris was assigned to the newly-created Special Trials Unit, where he remained for the next fourteen years successfully prosecuting numerous murder cases. In 1982, Norris convicted serial killer William Bonin of ten counts of first-degree murder with special circumstances; Bonin received the death penalty and was executed by lethal injection on February 23, 1996.

Norris retired from the District Attorney's Office in March 2000. He became the executive director of Judicial Watch, an organization that monitored judges in an attempt to prevent the miscarriage of justice in serious cases. Norris died on December 28, 2017.

PROSECUTION BRIEF

Prosecutor Norris recognized this was not a typical murder case. Almost every murder case involves an act by the perpetrator that directly causes the death, such as a shooting, stabbing or driving a vehicle while impaired. In this case, however, Donald Morse committed only the passive act of possessing a destructive device which did not detonate until after the police took custody of the device.

On August 26, 1986—six days before the preliminary hearing—Norris submitted to the court a legal brief titled, "Points and Authorities of First-Degree Murder and Special Circumstances." In the brief, Norris set forth the primary prosecution theories of first-degree murder, as follows:

> Penal Code section 189 provides first-degree murder in the following language:
>
> *"All murder which is perpetrated by means of a <u>destructive device</u> or <u>explosive</u>, knowing use of ammunition designed primarily to penetrate metal, poison, lying in wait, torture or by any other kind of willful, deliberate and premeditated killing . . . <u>is murder of the first-degree . . . .</u>" (Emphasis added.)*
>
> *Thus, the murders enumerated in Section 189 are first-degree murder as a matter of law. To come within this first-degree designation, it must be first established that the offense is a murder . . . Thus, if a killing can be established by normal means to be second-degree murder, Section 189 elevates that killing to first-degree. . . .*
>
> *Thus, if the killing of the two officers is shown to be second-degree murder as defined within the law, Section 189 elevates these crimes to first-degree murder.*
>
> *Second-degree murder can be established by two separate theories in this case. First, second-degree murder can be estab-*

lished by showing that the defendant was responsible for an act, "the natural consequences of which are dangerous to life, which act was deliberately performed by a person who knows that his conduct endangers the life of another and who acts with conscious disregard for life."

From the evidence adduced here, the defendant built and possessed the bomb. This conduct alone constitutes the implied malice for second-degree murder . . .

Secondly, murder, to qualify for the 189 elevation to first-degree murder, is also established in this case by second-degree felony murder. These killings taking place in the course of an inherently dangerous felony are by law second-degree murder. . . Certainly, possessing a destructive device such as a bomb would qualify as an inherently dangerous felony; what more inherently dangerous act is there than to build and possess a bomb?

Under either the theory of implied malice or the second-degree murder theory, murder is established and Section 189 by law elevates that to first-degree murder.

Under the prosecution's theory, Penal Code section 189 made the murder a second-degree murder and also elevated the murder to first-degree murder.

PRELIMINARY HEARING

On August 27, 1986, a preliminary hearing began in the case. What follows is an overview of the principals and the charges at the preliminary hearing:

PEOPLE v. DONALD LEE MORSE

Case A778741

JUDGE:	The Honorable Xenophon F. Lang
PROSECUTOR:	Sterling E. Norris, Deputy District Attorney
DEFENSE ATTORNEYS:	Pierpont Laidley, Attorney at Law
CHARGES:	Halvor Miller, Attorney at Law
	Count I - Murder of Arleigh McCree Count II - Murder of Ronald Ball
	Count III – Possession of Destructive Device in Residence
	Count IV - Possession of Destructive Device with Intent to Injure

Morse was held to answer on all charges on September 8, 1986, after a preliminary hearing that lasted seven days.

The pleading documents alleged special circumstances in that the defendant was responsible for the death of two victims. If Donald Morse were convicted of the two counts of first-degree murder with the special allegations found true, he would be eligible for the death penalty.

PROCEEDINGS BEFORE TRIAL

The trial was assigned to Judge John H. Major in the San Fernando Courthouse. Attorneys Pierpont Laidley and Halvor Miller continued to represent the defendant.

On November 1, 1986, the prosecution announced it would not seek the death penalty for Donald Morse. He now faced a maximum sentence of life in prison without the possibility of parole if convicted of first-degree murder with the special allegations found true. Morse remained in custody without bail.

On December 15, 1986, Judge John Major ruled that he would authorize the payment of county funds for only one lawyer to represent Donald Morse. Halvor Miller subsequently withdrew from the case as Pierpont Laidley continued to represent Morse, but now as his sole lawyer.

Over the next twelve months, Pierpont Laidley obtained numerous continuances of the trial despite the best efforts of prosecutor Sterling Norris to get the case to trial. Laidley would represent to the court that he was not ready for trial since he needed additional time to investigate and prepare the case. On December 28, 1987, as the case was approaching its second anniversary, Laidley appeared before Judge Major and once again requested a continuance stating that more investigation was necessary before he could be ready for trial. He asked for additional funds to conduct the investigation even though he had already received $143,000 at county expense to investigate the case. Judge Major then removed Pierpont Laidley as Morse's defense attorney stating, "you said you can't be ready for trial unless you are able to investigate the case further, and I am not going to give you more money to do that, so you're unavailable, and I am removing you." Judge Major appointed experienced defense attorney Bernard Rosen to represent Donald Morse.

Pierpont Laidley appealed his removal as Morse's defense lawyer, but the appellate court ruled that Judge Major did not abuse his discretion in removing Laidley from the case.

The substitution of Bernard Rosen as the defense attorney required several additional continuances so that he could become familiar with the case and get ready for trial.

JURY TRIAL

The jury trial finally began on February 21, 1989, with the start of jury selection. It was over three years since the deaths of Arleigh McCree and Ronald Ball. Below is an overview of the jury trial against Donald Morse.

PEOPLE v. DONALD LEE MORSE
Case A778741

JUDGE:	The Honorable John H. Major
PROSECUTOR:	Sterling E. Norris, Deputy District Attorney
DEFENSE ATTORNEY:	Bernard J. Rosen
	Court Appointed Defense Attorney
CHARGES:	Count I - Murder of Arleigh McCree
	Special Circumstances Alleged of Multiple Murder and Bomb Murder
	Count II - Murder of Ronald Ball
	Special Circumstances Alleged
	Count III - Possession of Destructive Device in Residence
	Count IV - Possession of Destructive Device with Intent to Injure
LOCATION:	Los Angeles Superior Court
	San Fernando Courthouse, Department A

SIGNIFICANT TRIAL DATES:

February 21, 1989:	Jury selection begins
March 13, 1989:	Opening statements
April 3, 1989:	Jury verdict
May 3, 1989:	Sentencing

During the trial, prosecutor Norris introduced evidence regarding the discovery of the bombs in Donald Morse's garage and Morse telling officers that he had never seen them before; the efforts by the victim officers to immobilize the bombs; and the recovery of various items in the garage and residence that strongly indicated that Morse was in possession of the bombs and had probably constructed them. Expert witnesses testified to the construction of the bombs and that the bombs were designed to kill human beings.

William Enoch testified that he was married to Donald Morse's sister, Ernestine. Enoch and Ernestine lived in Orlando, Florida, with their three children. In September 1985, Ernestine left Mr. Enoch and took the children with her to California where they stayed with Donald Morse at his residence on Vanscoy Avenue in North Hollywood. On Sunday, January 24, 1986, Morse telephoned Enoch and told him to send money to take care of his children. Enoch refused, and Morse told him, "Well, I don't appreciate people messing with my family. I have connections in Orlando, and I can make your life miserable. I'll blow you up in your car." Enoch telephoned the North Hollywood station of the Los Angeles Police Department and reported the threat. Two weeks later, Officers Arleigh McCree and Ronald Ball died in Morse's garage when the bomb they were attempting to immobilize exploded.

Al Ward was a neighbor and friend of Donald Morse. Sometime in October 1978, Ward was in Morse's garage when Morse showed up with a book with descriptions of how to make a bomb (the book was not "The Anarchist Cookbook"). Morse told Ward, "I can make a bomb."

Defense attorney Bernard Rosen attempted to introduce evidence on the issue of causation, i.e., that the death of the two officers was not a reasonable and foreseeable consequence of the defendant's possession of the bomb. Rosen sought to call an expert witness on bombs to testify that the bombs could have been safely moved to another location and rendered safe by remote means. Judge Major excluded the offered evidence as not relevant.

Rosen also attempted to introduce evidence that the officers' actions inside the garage and their failure to take safety precautions contributed to their deaths. However, Judge John Major ruled out any such testimony.

Donald Morse did not testify at the trial. Instead, he relied on statements he had made to the police that he had no knowledge the bombs were in his garage.

FINAL ARGUMENTS AND JURY VERDICT

Since the prosecution has the burden of proving the defendant's guilt to a unanimous jury beyond a reasonable doubt, it has the benefit of making both the opening and closing arguments to the jury. The defense is permitted only one closing argument.

On March 29, 1989, prosecutor Sterling Norris gave his opening argument to the jury. The following day, defense attorney Bernard Rosen made his argument to the jury and then Norris gave his closing argument. Norris concluded by telling the jury that it all boiled down to who possessed the bomb when the officers arrived at the defendant's residence:

> *"No question. You have to decide whose bomb that is. Did he possess that bomb, or is it like he said: Well, gee whiz, I don't know what that is?*
>
> *"It's as simple as that. If he's the bomber, he's guilty of first-degree murder on both counts, guilty with the special circumstances and guilty of the possession of the destruction device. Thank you." (Trial transcript, pages 874-875.)*

On April 4, 1989, the jury convicted Donald Lee Morse of the two counts of first-degree murder and one count of reckless or malicious possession of a destructive device and found true alleged special circumstances of multiple murder and murder by destructive device.

On May 3, 1989, Judge John Major denied the defense motion for a new trial and for reduction of verdict. He then sentenced Donald Morse to life in prison without the possibility of parole.

APPELLATE COURT DECISION

On January 9, 1992, a three-judge panel of the California Court of Appeal issued its decision in Donald Morse's appeal of his conviction and sentence. The opinion appears in the Official California reports as *People v. Morse* (1992) 2 Cal. App. 4th 620.

In a 2-1 decision, the majority affirmed the murder convictions, but it reduced the degree of the murder from first-degree to second-degree murder. It held that the reckless or malicious possession of a destructive device was an inherently dangerous felony and that a killing taking place in the course of an inherently dangerous felony was second-degree murder under the felony murder rule. However, the majority then held that the trial judge committed error in instructing the jurors that they could use the crime of possession of a destructive device twice, first to find that the defendant committed second-degree murder, and second to convert that murder into murder of the first degree.[2]

The dissenting judge in his opinion questioned whether the second-degree felony murder applied. His conclusion contained the following language:

> *"Contrary to prior California law, the majority opinion holds possession of a dangerous object, without any act or intent to use the object, can supply the predicate for a felony-murder conviction. The opinion then lays a felony-murder curse on the possessor which does not go away even after the felony has terminated, the possessor no longer has possession, and the state has assumed complete dominion of the device...*
>
> *". . . I would reverse this conviction."* (People v. Morse, 2 Cal.App.4th at pages 673, 674.)

---

[2] *This was the legal theory for first-degree murder advanced by the prosecution in its legal brief dated August 26, 1986, submitted to the court before the preliminary hearing.*

The petitions of both the prosecution and the defense for review by the California Supreme Court were denied on April 16, 1992. As a result, the decision by the Court of Appeal became final and binding on the parties.

RE-SENTENCING

On October 7, 1992, Donald Lee Morse appeared before Judge John Major for resentencing. The prosecution was still represented by Sterling Norris, and Morse was now represented by private attorney Arthur Goldberg.

Judge Major vacated the previous sentence imposed on May 3, 1989. Since the defendant was now guilty of two counts of second-degree murder as a result of the Court of Appeal decision, Judge Major imposed a sentence of fifteen years to life as to Count 1, plus fifteen years to life as to Count 2, for a total of thirty years to life. Morse was given credit for eleven years and nine months in custody (eighty-two months actual custody and fifty-nine months good time and work time credits).

PAROLE CONSIDERATION HEARING

With the sentence of thirty-years to life, Donald Lee Morse became eligible for parole. His first (and only) parole consideration hearing took place on January 28, 2006, at the Vacaville State Prison. Deputy District Attorney Michael Montagna represented the prosecution by videoconference from Los Angeles, and attorney Michael J. Gunning was personally present with inmate Morse at the hearing.

The three-person panel denied parole to Donald Morse based on the seriousness of the commitment offense and an unfavorable psychiatric report. A rehearing was set for five years. Deputy District Attorney Montagna prepared a memorandum of the hearing and made the following comments:

> "*This inmate had the opportunity to save the officers' lives if he had spoken up when the bombs were found. They pointed them out to him, and he said he had never seen them. The construction of the bombs and the way they were triggered made them a disaster waiting to happen. They were designed for one purpose only, to kill, according to the expert who testified at trial. The inmate blames his trial attorneys and the justice system for his conviction. He has no remorse. He is cold, calculating, articulate and manipulative.*"

EPILOGUE – DONALD LEE MORSE

While confined in state prison, the health of Donald Lee Morse began to deteriorate in 2004, when he was diagnosed with a brain tumor. He underwent surgery to excise a tumor (benign) in the left temporal lobe in November 2004. At the time of his parole consideration hearing in January 19, 2006, Morse was still recovering from the surgery.

Morse had a history of seizure disorders and migraine headaches, for which he was taking medication. He also had degenerative disk disease and arthritis is his hips. Often, he used a wheelchair because of his mobility problems.

Donald Lee Morse died on May 1, 2009, at age fifty-nine while incarcerated in the California state prison.

LESSONS LEARNED

"The Hurt Locker" won the Oscar for the Best Motion Picture of 2011. It portrayed the actions of bomb dismantlers in the war in Iraq. There are few activities that are more dangerous than dismantling a live bomb. In the movie, the bomb experts wore body armor that at least provided a chance of survival if the bomb exploded while it was being dismantled.

Some persons are just too brave for their own good. Detective McCree and Officer Ball were assigned to the Firearms and Explosives Unit of the Los Angeles Police Department. Part of the job was the dismantling of live bombs which was done without the protection of body armor. Both officers died when a bomb exploded while it was being dismantled.

The Firearms and Explosives Unit has changed its policy in the dismantling of bombs. Now these destructive devices are photographed in the location where they are discovered. Then they are carefully moved to a location where they are detonated under controlled conditions.

Arleigh McCree

Date of Birth:	December 24, 1939
Date Appointed:	February, 1965
End of Watch:	February 8, 1986

Ronald Ball

Date of Birth:	December 12, 1942
Date Appointed:	August, 1969
End of Watch:	February 8, 1986

Memorial street sign at 6800 block of Vanscoy Avenue, North Hollywood

Photos Courtesy of Jimmy Trahin

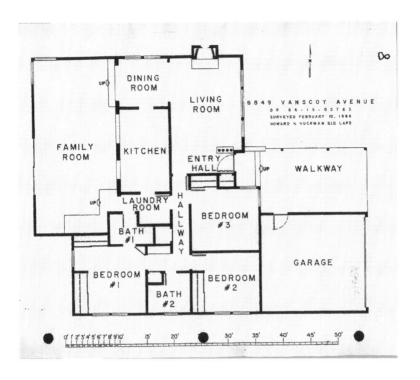

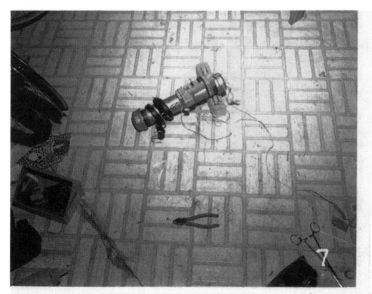

One of the two pipe bombs discovered in suspect's garage

Photographic sequence as bomb explodes in suspect's garage

Garage after bodies of officers have been removed

Explosive demonstration at Sheriff's bomb range on September 30, 1987

CHAPTER THREE

Officers James MacDonald and Kevin Burrell

Compton Police Department

"Don't Let Your Guard Down"

February 23, 1993

JAMES WAYNE MacDONALD

JAMES WAYNE MACDONALD was born on November 4, 1968, in Santa Rosa, California. He was the second of two sons born to James and Tonia MacDonald. James was about two years younger than his brother, Jon, and they grew up as best friends in a close-knit family.

Through high school, James "Jimmy" MacDonald was active in sports. In his senior year, he was named all-league quarterback in football and an all-league point guard in basketball. He was also selected to the all-star baseball team.

After graduating from high school, he attended Cal State University Long Beach. He graduated in 1992 with a Bachelor of Arts degree, having majored in communications with a minor in criminal justice. MacDonald had wanted to be a police officer for a long time; and in June 1991, he became a reserve officer for the Compton Police Department. For his senior year in college, he was able to complete his college education while working part-time as a police officer.

MacDonald wanted to become a full-time police officer, but Compton did not have the resources to hire any more officers. He sent resumes to several police agencies; he was hired by the San Jose Police Department to begin as a full-time officer effective March 8, 1992. MacDonald was excited about the new job, since he would be a full-time officer and would be living near his family and friends in the Santa Rosa area. He rented an apartment in the San Jose area in preparation for his new employment.

MacDonald remained in Los Angeles to complete his last two tours for the Compton Police Department. His last tour of duty was on the evening shift from 4:00 p.m. to 1:30 a.m. beginning February 22, 1993. He was shot and killed on that date with just a few hours remaining in his last shift as a Compton police officer.

KEVIN MICHAEL BURRELL

Kevin Michael Burrell was born on May 5, 1963, in Los Angeles, California. He was one of seven children born to Clark and Edna Burrell. Kevin Burrell grew up in Compton and attended Compton High School where he played on the basketball team.

In high school, Kevin was interested in becoming a police officer. He became an Explorer Scout at the age of fifteen for the Compton Police Department. He attended Cal State University, Dominguez Hills, where he was a starter on the basketball team.

Burrell joined the Compton Police Department on July 3, 1988, at the age of 25. He was a giant African-American male at 6 feet 5 inches and 300 pounds, and he was known as "Big Kev." He wanted to help young people and spoke at schools to students about the dangers of drugs and gangs, and the importance of going to school. Sometimes he would counsel a person whom he had detained, rather than arresting him; he felt good that he had given that person another chance.

Kevin Burrell and James MacDonald were close friends. On the afternoon of February 22, 1993, they had dinner at Burrell's house, prepared by Burrell's mother, to celebrate MacDonald's last night of duty for the Compton Police Department. On the late evening of February 22, 1993, Burrell and MacDonald were shot and killed in the line of duty.

REGIS DEON THOMAS

Regis Deon Thomas was born on October 18, 1970. Growing up, he never knew his father and lived with his mother, two sisters, and two brothers. When Thomas was ten-years-old, his mother's boyfriend moved into the house and acted as a father. However, the boyfriend moved out after two years, largely because Thomas' mother was addicted to cocaine.

Thomas was a member of the "Bounty Hunters," a street gang based in the Nickerson Gardens Housing Project. He had several encounters with the police prior to February 22, 1993. All of them involved the possession and/or use of a firearm. These encounters included:

- On October 1, 1988, he was arrested in possession of a Smith and Wesson revolver. He was convicted of unlawful possession of a firearm.

- On February 16, 1990, Thomas was arrested by the Los Angeles Housing Authority in possession of a Taurus .38 caliber revolver. He was convicted of battery and unlawful possession of a firearm.

- On May 23, 1992, Thomas was arrested for the murder of Carlos Atkins, who was shot in the chest on January 31, 1992, in front of three eyewitnesses. At the time of his arrest, he was driving a red 1992 Chevrolet pickup truck. A loaded Smith and Wesson 9-millimeter pistol between the driver's seat and center console was recovered by the arresting officers. Thomas remained in custody until the murder charges were dismissed on October 7, 1992, after one of the eyewitnesses to the murder (Andre Chappell) was shot and killed on March 20, 1992. A second eyewitness (Bertrand Dickson) signed a statement for the defense stating, "I am sure now that I made a mistake . . ." in identifying Regis Thomas as the shooter. The third witness (Janice Chappell) was not available for the trial.

FEBRUARY 22, 1993

On February 22, 1993, in the late evening hours, Officer Kevin Burrell and Reserve Officer James MacDonald of the Compton Police Department were on patrol during the 4:00 p.m. to 1:30 a.m. shift. They were both in uniform in a marked police vehicle.

Between 11:00 and 11:15 p.m., they stopped a red Chevrolet pickup truck for a traffic violation. The location of the stop was Rosecrans Avenue just east of Dwight Avenue. Since Rosecrans Avenue was a major street in the city of Compton, there were several eyewitness accounts of what happened during the traffic stop, mostly from Margaretta Hays Gully and the occupants of her vehicle.

Margaretta Hays Gully

Margaretta Hays Gully was a 40-year-old African-American female. On February 22, 1993, at approximately 11:10 p.m., she was driving her white 1966 Chevrolet Caprice westbound on Rosecrans Avenue in the right-hand lane going to pick up her eighteen-year-old son, Deshon, who worked at a Blockbuster Video Store on Rosecrans Avenue just east of Central Avenue. Her twelve-year-old son, Demoryea Polidore, was in the front seat and her eleven-year-old daughter, Ebony Gully, and her older son's girlfriend, Alicia Jordan, were in the back seat. Through the windshield of her car, Ms. Gully saw two police officers, one black and one white, struggling with a suspect. The African-American officer had the African-American suspect by the right arm and the white officer had the suspect by the left arm. It appeared to her that the officers were attempting to arrest the suspect and put his arms behind his back. A red pickup truck was parked nearby with the door open on the driver's side. As Ms. Gully passed the scene, she heard a series of gunshots fired. Through her rearview mirror, she saw the suspect straddling one of the officers, who was on the ground. Her son, Demoryea, yelled, "They're shooting the cops! They're shooting the cops in the head!" Alicia Jordan stated that the pickup truck was coming after them. Ms. Gully got to the Blockbuster Video Store and observed the truck make a rapid right turn from Rosecrans Avenue onto Central Avenue.

The occupants of Ms. Gully's vehicle gave similar statements. Demoryea observed that the red pickup had "4x4" or "454" over the rear wheels. Alicia Jordan stated that she saw the word "Chevrolet" on the tailgate of the pickup truck.

Ms. Gully was concerned about her safety and that of her passengers. She did not notify the police of her observations until February 24, 1993. In her statement, she stated that her vehicle was within five to eight feet of the officers and the suspect as she drove by the location. The area was lit up by the red lights flashing, spotlights, and headlights. Ms. Gully and the occupants in her car stated that they could not positively identify the shooter, but they were able to describe his general features and body type as an African-American male, twenty-one to twenty-six years of age, short hair, clean shaven, with an athletic build.

CRIME SCENE

The intersection of Rosecrans Avenue and Dwight Avenue was controlled by tri-phase traffic control lights, one on all four corners. There were overhanging traffic control lights on the southeast corner of the intersection. Rosecrans Avenue had four lanes of travel, two for eastbound traffic and two for westbound travel. Double, solid yellow lines separated the east and westbound lanes, and broken white lines separated the lanes going in the same direction.

The first Compton police vehicle at the scene in response to a "Code 9, Officer Down" radio call arrived at 11:20 p.m. Police Unit 20, used by Officers Burrell and MacDonald, was located in the right-hand lane of Rosecrans Avenue, facing westbound, just before Dwight Avenue. The police vehicle's engine was running, the keys were in the ignition, and the driver's door was slightly ajar. Officer Burrell was lying face down in a large pool of blood near the front passenger side of the police vehicle. Officer MacDonald was lying on his back in a large pool of blood near the front driver's side of the police vehicle.

Officers Burrell and MacDonald were in police uniform with their service weapons still in their holsters. Both officers had received multiple gunshot wounds, including a gunshot wound to the head. They were transported to Martin Luther King Hospital, where they were pronounced dead upon arrival.

AUTOPSIES
Kevin Burrell

On February 24, 1993, an autopsy on the body of Officer Kevin Burrell was performed by Dr. James Wegner of the Los Angeles County Coroner's Office. The clothing worn by Officer Burrell included a bulletproof vest. Dr. Wegner ascribed the cause of death to "multiple gunshot wounds." He determined that Officer Burrell had sustained four bullet wounds, described in the autopsy report:

1. Fatal gunshot wound of head.
2. Gunshot wound through left chin area and into left chest wall.
3. Gunshot wound of right upper arm.
4. Non-fatal gunshot wound through left foot and lower leg. This wound was consistent with the officer being on his back on the ground and lifting his foot to fend off a shot.

The bullet from wound number two, and bullet fragments from wounds one and three were recovered during the autopsy. Although the cause of death was ascribed to multiple gunshot wounds, Dr. Wegner opined ". . . the head wound that is gunshot wound one being by far the most responsible for the death."

James MacDonald

Dr. James Ribe of the Los Angeles County Coroner's Office performed the autopsy of the body of Officer James MacDonald on February 25, 1993. Officer MacDonald's clothing included a bulletproof vest. Dr. Ribe ascribed the cause of death to "gunshot wound of the back." He described in the autopsy report four gunshot wounds that Officer MacDonald sustained, as:

- Gunshot wound one perforating intermediate range, back-to-front, low-velocity wound of the right side of the head. Nonfatal.

- Gunshot wound two a penetrating back-to-front, low-velocity wound of the neck. Bullet recovered in the retropharyngeal space.

- Gunshot wound three a superficial impact wound of the left mid-back. The wound is shored. It only penetrates dermis.

- Gunshot wound four a fatal perforating back-to-front, low-velocity wound of the back.
  - Entrance left from lower back.
  - Exit left axilla.
  - Course through the back, left kidney, tail of pancreas, spleen, stomach, omentum, diaphragm, lung, chest wall.
  - Direction back-to-front, superior and right to left.

The bullet from wound two was recovered during the autopsy and transferred to the custody of the detectives in the autopsy room. The cause of death was gunshot wound four.

INVESTIGATION

The murder of two Compton police officers would require an in-depth and extensive investigation that a small police agency such as the Compton Police Department would be unable to conduct. The Compton Police Department asked the Los Angeles County Sheriff's Department to handle the investigation. The Sheriff's Department had over 5,000 sworn personnel and a Detective Division that included a Homicide Bureau, consisting of skilled and experienced detectives specializing in the investigation of murder cases.

On February 26, 1993, the Compton Homicide Task Force was created, consisting of one lieutenant, one administrative sergeant, and over twenty deputies from the Sheriff's OSS detail. They worked in conjunction with Compton Police Department personnel investigating incoming clues. The Sheriff's Department provided the manpower, and Compton officers provided street intelligence from the Compton community. During the course of the investigation, over 500 clues were investigated and evaluated.

On February 27, 1993, Sheriff's investigators conducted detailed, tape-recorded interviews of Margaretta Gully and her twelve-year-old son, Demoryea Polidore. This gave the investigators an excellent overview of the circumstances of the crime, but it was insufficient to establish the actual identity of the suspect.

On February 28, 1993, Detectives Ron Duval and Alex MacArthur of the Compton Homicide Task Force began investigating Regis Thomas as a possible suspect. They determined that he was a member of the Bounty Hunters street gang with ties to the Nickerson Gardens Housing Project. He had an extensive record involving possession of firearms and had possible involvement in the murders of Carlos Atkins and Andre Chappell. He was the owner of a Chevrolet pickup truck similar to the one used in the murder.

On March 1, 1993, Detectives Duval and MacArthur drove to the residence of Regis Thomas in San Pedro. In front of the location, they observed a bright red 1992 Chevrolet 454 pickup truck with stock tires and rims and tinted windows. Thomas was not at the location; the detectives spoke to Ms. Deshaunna Cody. She told the detectives that she lived there with her boyfriend, Regis Thomas, and their four small children. She stated that the red pickup truck was a gift from her relatives for graduating from high school and that Regis Thomas regularly used the truck. When asked where the truck was on the night of the murders, Cody stated that they were all home by 8:00 p.m. since they were "always" in the house by

8:00 p.m. The detectives obtained a photograph of Regis Thomas from Deshaunna Cody and terminated the interview.

On March 4, 1993, Detectives Duval and MacArthur located Regis Thomas and interviewed him. Thomas stated that he and his girlfriend, Deshaunna Cody, used a red 1992 Chevrolet 454 pickup truck. He said that he could not remember where he was on the evening of February 22, 1993, but thought he was at home with Deshaunna in San Pedro because he was usually in for the night by 8:00 p.m. When asked if he had heard anything about the murders of the Compton officers, Thomas replied, "No, man. That night when them cops got killed, I'm glad I was here in the projects with my truck and not out on the street." The interview was then terminated.

RECOVERY OF MURDER WEAPON

The investigation went on for weeks without identifying the killer of the Compton police officers. The big break in the case came after Calvin Cooksey was arrested on March 22, 1993, by deputies from the West Hollywood Sheriff's Station for unlawful possession of a firearm. Charges were filed against Cooksey in the Beverly Hills courthouse. Cooksey was a street hustler with a lengthy arrest record; he had worked with Sheriff's Deputy Larry Brandenberg in the past as an informant.

On the morning of March 25, 1993, Detective Brandenberg received a collect call from Calvin Cooksey, who was in custody at the Men's Central Jail. Cooksey stated that he had information regarding the murder of the two Compton police officers. That afternoon, Detective Brandenberg and his partner Detective Michael Costleigh went to the Men's Central Jail to interview Calvin Cooksey.

Cooksey told the detectives that "Reggie," or Regis Thomas, from the street gang "Bounty Hunter Bloods" killed the two Compton police officers. After shooting the officers, Reggie left the handgun (a nine-millimeter automatic) at a girlfriend's house. A day or two later, Reggie asked

Cooksey if he wanted a handgun, and Cooksey agreed to accept the weapon. Reggie arranged for the girlfriend to give Cooksey the weapon. Cooksey drove to the girlfriend's house near 108th Street and Juniper Avenue and knocked on the front door. An African-American female opened the door and handed Cooksey a brown paper bag, which contained a nine-millimeter automatic handgun. Later that evening Cooksey sold the handgun for $260 to a male Hispanic named Robert.

Cooksey went on to say that on the following day, he was at his cousin Phillip Cathcart's apartment when Reggie arrived. They were watching television, and the news was broadcasting information that the vehicle involved in the murder of the Compton officers was a red pickup truck. According to Cooksey, Reggie stated, "Yes, I killed the mother fuckers. They were slippen motherfuckers. Didn't even get their guns out." Reggie described the shootings in detail and stated that the gun he had given Cooksey was the murder weapon. Reggie said that after shooting the officers, he jumped into his truck and sped away. He drove to his girlfriend's house in San Pedro and left his truck there. He was staying at his friend Phillip Cathcart's house for about a week until things cooled down.

Deputies Brandenberg and Costleigh told Detectives Duval and MacArthur about the information that they had received from Calvin Cooksey. Since Duval and MacArthur had been working Regis Thomas from the start, it was agreed that they would follow up on Cooksey's information.

On March 31, 1993, Detectives Duval and MacArthur interviewed Calvin Cooksey at the Men's Central Jail. Cooksey repeated the information that he had previously given to Detectives Brandenberg and Costleigh. However, this time he added that he could buy the gun back from Robert if he was out of jail. Later, Cooksey identified a booking photo of Robert Rojas as depicting the person to whom he had sold the gun.

On the morning April 1, 1993, the Sheriff's deputies arranged for the release of Calvin Cooksey on his own recognizance on his pending case in the Beverly Hills Municipal Court. On April 1, Cooksey and Compton Police Officer William Jackson (acting in an undercover capacity) met with Robert Rojas and discussed buying back the gun. Rojas stated that one of his "homeboys" had the gun and that he would not be able to get ahold of his homeboy until the following day. Rojas told Cooksey to page him tomorrow afternoon, and he would have the gun, which Rojas had loaned to another gang member.

On the afternoon of April 2, 1993, members of the Compton Homicide Task Force investigating the murders of Compton Officers Burrell and MacDonald organized an operation to recover the murder weapon.

Detective Tim Miley, a deputy sheriff assigned to the Task Force, described the operation as follows:

Detective Miley had written a search warrant for the Rojas residence in case something went wrong with the purchase. The Task Force had access to an undercover van that was used in gang operations. It was a beat-up Chevrolet van with tinted windows on each side and a curtain separating the cargo area from the driver. It was disguised to look like a painter's van.

In the van that day were undercover Officer Jackson, Calvin Cooksey, Detective Miley, and three other officers. Detective Miley and one of the officers were armed with shotguns. The van was driven by Detective Solomon Patton, an experienced African American detective who was about fifty years of age at the time. There were some black and white chase cars parked a few blocks away.

Detective Patton parked the van across the street and a few houses south of the Rojas house. Undercover Officer Jackson and Calvin Cooksey exited the van and went to the Rojas house. Several houses away there was a small group of Blood gang members who were apparently selling drugs. Two of them walked up to the van, one on each side, with several others following. One of the men went to Patton and told him to get out of the van so they could see what was inside. The person talking had a blue steel pistol in his waistband. Detective Miley had his shotgun trained on him as soon as he saw the gun. Miley heard the officer with the shotgun whisper that the guy on the passenger side also had a gun. He trained his shotgun on that man. The officers were concerned that a gunfight might take place, which could endanger Cooksey and the undercover officer who were inside a nearby residence involved in a dangerous undercover gun buy.

The stalemate went on for several minutes with Patton refusing to let the gangsters look in the van, telling them that he was a painter and that his livelihood was invested in his painting equipment. The gang members became more aggressive. The man talking to Patton was now holding the gun by his side. Detective Miley's shotgun was only a few inches from his head, behind the mirrored glass. Suddenly, one of the men whistled, and they retreated to the rear of the van. They had a short conversation and took off running. Apparently, they figured out that this was the police.

About five minutes later, Cooksey and Officer Jackson returned to the van with a gun, which Cooksey had purchased from Robert Rojas for $350. The gun was a Sig Sauer nine-millimeter semi-automatic pistol.

Sheriff's investigators took possession of the gun and transported it to the Sheriff's Crime Lab for ballistic examination by Deputy Dwight Van Horne, a recognized ballistics expert. Deputy Van Horne stated that the cartridge casings found at the scene of the shootings of the officers were fired from the gun.

The murder weapon had been stolen in Las Vegas on February 8, 1993, in a burglary of the Active Sports Gun Store. A total of forty-six guns were stolen in this burglary.

SERVICE OF SEARCH WARRANTS

With the recovery of the murder weapon, Regis Leon Thomas was now identified as the person who had shot and killed Compton police officers Kevin Burrell and James MacDonald. However, determining the identity of a suspect does not necessarily mean that there is sufficient admissible evidence to convict that person in a court of law. The investigators now focused on developing additional evidence that could be used in a jury trial against Regis Thomas.

April 6, 1993 was targeted as the date that Thomas would be arrested, and searches would be conducted of residences connected to him. On that date, search warrants were served at several locations, including the following:

- 107 North Beacon Street, San Pedro. Twenty-one-year-old Deshaunna Tranise Cody shared this residence with Regis Thomas and their four children. Thomas was not home when the search warrant was served, but Cody was at the residence. A Firestar nine-millimeter handgun was found in her purse. She admitted that Thomas had given her the gun approximately two weeks ago. This gun had been stolen in the same Las Vegas burglary on February 8, 1993, as the murder weapon.

- 1830 West El Segundo Boulevard, Apartment 3, Gardena. This was the residence of Phillip Cathcart, the cousin of Calvin Cooksey, and a close associate of Regis Thomas. A Glock nine-millimeter handgun was recovered from this location. This gun was also stolen in the same Las Vegas burglary as the murder weapon. Phillip Cathcart refused to make a statement or otherwise cooperate with the investigators.

Regis Thomas, who had not been home during the service of the search warrants, surrendered at the Carson Sheriff's Station later in the day on April 6, 1993.

DEPUTY DISTRICT ATTORNEY MARK ARNOLD

In 1993, co-author Robert Schirn was the head deputy overseeing the Special Crimes Division. One of the sections over which he had oversight was the Crimes Against Peace Officers Section (CAPOS). This section was responsible for assisting the police in investigating, and later prosecuting, defendants charged with serious assaults and murders of police officers.

After the murders of Compton police officers Kevin Burrell and James MacDonald, Deputy District Attorney Mark Arnold was assigned to assist the Compton Homicide Task Force in its investigation. Arnold attended the autopsies of the officers and provided legal advice and assistance during the course of the investigation.

Arnold was born in New York City in 1948. In 1960, the family moved to West Los Angeles. He attended Palisades High School and was the 1966 Los Angeles All-City champion shot putter.

Mark Arnold had the ideal background for a prosecutor in CAPOS. He had joined the Los Angeles County Sheriff's Department in 1972 and spent the next thirteen years as a deputy sheriff. He went to law school at night, passed the state bar examination, and joined the District Attorney's Office in 1985 as an entry-level prosecutor. He proved to be an excellent trial lawyer. He successfully prosecuted serious gang cases as a member of the Hardcore Gang Division. In 1990, he obtained the assignment that he most wanted, and became a member of CAPOS.

In 1998, Governor Pete Wilson appointed Mark Arnold to the Los Angeles Superior Court, where he has served with distinction as a Superior Court Judge. Arnold has had three significant careers, first as a law enforcement officer, then as a prosecutor, and finally as a judge.

Among his outstanding accomplishments as a deputy district attorney was the prosecution of Regis Thomas for the murders of Compton police officers Kevin Burrell and James MacDonald.

FILING OF CHARGES

On April 7, 1993, Deputy District Attorney Mark Arnold filed the following charges against Regis Deon Thomas:

- Count one -- Murder of Carlos Atkins with use of a firearm.

- Count two -- Murder of Compton police officer Kevin Burrell with use of a firearm.

- Count three -- Murder of Compton police officer James MacDonald with use of a firearm.

- Counts four and five -- Felon in possession of a firearm.

Special circumstances were alleged that (1) the officers were killed while engaged in the performance of their duties, and (2) the defendant committed more than one murder. If either special circumstance were found true by the jury, it would make Regis Thomas eligible for the death penalty.

In filing these charges against Regis Thomas, prosecutor Mark Arnold made the tactical decision to include the murder of Carlos Atkins, even though this murder had been previously charged against Thomas and later dismissed. California Penal Code section 954 permits joinder of "two or more different offenses of the same class of crimes or offenses." This requirement was clearly met in the case against Regis Thomas since the first three counts all alleged murder.

If the murder of Carlos Atkins remained in the accusatory pleading, the jury would hear evidence against Thomas of two separate incidents involving the killing of human beings rather than just one.

ASSIGNMENT FOR TRIAL

The case against Regis Thomas proceeded through a preliminary hearing without incident. The trial was assigned to Judge Edward A. Ferns for trial. What follows is an overview of the principals in the case.

PEOPLE v. REGIS DEON THOMAS
Case BA075063

JUDGE: The Honorable Edward A. Ferns
PROSECUTOR: Mark Arnold, Deputy District Attorney
DEFENSE ATTORNEYS: Jay Jaffe, Attorney at Law
                        Victoria Doherty, Attorney at Law

CHARGES: Count I -- Murder of Carlos Atkins with use of a firearm
                        Count II -- Murder of Compton police officer Kevin Burrell with use of a firearm
                        Count III -- Murder of Compton police officer James MacDonald with use of a firearm
                        Counts IV and V -- Felon in possession of a firearm

LOCATION OF TRIAL: Los Angeles Superior Court
                        Central District, Department 106
                        Criminal Courts Building [later, the Clara Shortridge Foltz Criminal Justice Center], Downtown Los Angeles

PRE-TRIAL MOTION TO SEVER
CARLOS ATKINS MURDER CHARGE

Defense attorney Jay Jaffe recognized that the inclusion of the murder charge for Carlos Atkins along with the murder charges involving the two police officers greatly strengthened the People's case to the detriment of his client. Jaffe made a pre-trial motion to sever the Carlos Atkins murder count and have it prosecuted in a separate trial. If the severance motion were granted, the jury hearing the trial of the two officers would not learn of the Atkins murder except during a possible penalty phase.

Jaffe argued that failure to sever the Carlos Atkins murder charge would deprive his client of his right to receive a fair trial. Jaffe indicated there was a possibility Regis Thomas might testify regarding self-defense in the trial of the Atkins homicide; but he would not testify in connection with the police officer counts.

Judge Edward Ferns found the joinder of the three murder charges was proper under California Penal Code section 954, and he denied the defense motion to sever.

JURY TRIAL – MURDER OF CARLOS ATKINS

Prosecutor Mark Arnold presented the People's evidence in chronological order. First, he called witnesses on the murder of Carlos Atkins alleged in Count I of the information. On January 31, 1992, at approximately 2:00 a.m., Carlos Atkins was shot to death inside the residence of Andre and Janice Chappell at the Nickerson Gardens Housing Projects. Three persons – Andre and Janice Chappell, and a visitor to their apartment named Bertrand Dickson – observed the incident. Regis Thomas had previously been charged with the murder of Carlos Atkins, but Andre Chappell was shot and killed by an unknown assailant before the preliminary hearing in the case. Bertrand Dickson then claimed that he had incorrectly identified Regis Thomas as the shooter, and Janice Chappell could not make a positive identification. This case against Regis Thomas was dismissed for insufficient evidence to proceed to trial.

In the instant trial, Deputy District Attorney Mark Arnold called the two surviving witnesses in the shooting death of Carlos Atkins, as follows:

Bertrand Dickson

In the early morning hours of January 31, 1992, he was visiting his friend Andre Chappell at his apartment in the Nickerson Gardens Housing Projects. Dickson briefly left the apartment to buy some cigarettes. Upon his return, he thought he heard someone calling his nickname, "Lucky." Believing it to be his friend "Romeo," Dickson called out "Romeo, down here." Regis Thomas was driving by, and he called out to Dickson, "You don't know me, don't try to sell me anything." Dickson explained that he had not been talking to Thomas, and he walked to the Chappells' apartment.

Dickson entered the apartment and observed Carlos Atkins and Andre Chappell in the living room. Someone banged on the front door, which was opened by Chappell. Regis Thomas entered carrying a gun by his side, and he made some angry remarks. Dickson again explained that he was calling out to his friend Romeo and was not trying to sell anything to Thomas. At this time, Thomas started to leave the apartment as he walked toward the door. He noticed Janice Chappell walking down the stairs and apologized to her for the disturbance and stated that the men in the apartment "don't know who I am." Carlos Atkins then stated to Thomas, "You don't know who I am either." Thomas came back into the apartment, placed the gun at Atkins' head, and threatened to blow his brains out. Atkins grabbed the gun, and a struggle ensued. Two shots were fired, one striking Atkins in the chest.

Dickson ran to another apartment and called 911. While he was waiting for the ambulance, Thomas and another man approached him. They told him not to say anything about the incident and hit him with the gun.

The two men tried to get Dickson into the trunk of their car, but he was able to run away.

Bertrand Dickson later met with police detectives and described the circumstances of the shooting. He identified Thomas as the shooter in a photographic lineup and later selected him in a live lineup.

A few months later, in September 1992, Dickson was in custody on burglary charges. He was transported to the Compton courthouse for Regis Thomas' upcoming trial on the Atkins murder. Dickson was placed in a holding cell with Regis Thomas, who asked him why he was going to testify. Thomas told Dickson that he didn't want to end up like Andre (Chappell). Dickson was aware that Chappell had been shot to death. Dickson then told the prosecutor that he had identified the wrong man, and the murder charge against Thomas was dismissed.

In the instant case, Bertrand Dickson positively identified the defendant Regis Thomas as the person who shot Carlos Atkins. He admitted to seven prior felony convictions and testified that he was promised that he could serve his sentence on his pending burglary charge outside Los Angeles County.

Janice Chappell

She testified that on the early morning of January 31, 1992, she was living with her husband, Andre Chappell, in an apartment in the Nickerson Gardens Housing Projects. She was awakened by the sounds of arguing and walked out of her bedroom and down the stairs. She observed her husband, Andre Chappell, Carlos Atkins, Bertrand Dickson, and a man with a gun in the living room. The man with the gun appeared angry, and her husband appeared to be trying to calm him down. The man with the gun was leaving the apartment and apologized to her for the disturbance, saying that the men in the apartment did not know who he was. Carlos Atkins then stated to the man with the gun that he did not know who he (Atkins) was. The man came back into the apartment, placed the gun at

Atkins' head, threatened him and fired two shots. Atkins was shot in the chest, and the man with the gun left the apartment. She did not see a struggle between Atkins and the man with the gun before the shots were fired.

On February 25, 1992, Janice Chappell selected Regis Thomas' photograph from a photographic display, indicating that he looked like the man who shot Carlos Atkins. At the instant trial, Chappell testified that she was ninety-eight percent sure Regis Thomas was the man who shot Atkins. She stated that the only reason she was not one-hundred percent sure was because she had never seen him before.

Coroner's testimony

Dr. Pedro M. Ortiz-Colom of the Los Angeles County Coroner's Office performed the autopsy on the body of Carlos Atkins on February 1, 1992. He described Atkins as a 39-year-old black male, 5 feet 3 inches tall, weighing 133 pounds. He ascribed the cause of death to a "gunshot wound to chest."

JURY TRIAL
Murders of Officers Burrell AND MacDonald

The evidence prosecutor Mark Arnold presented to the jury to prove that Regis Thomas murdered the two officers fell into five different categories, as follows:

1. *Margaretta Gully and the occupants of her car.* Margaretta Gully, her twelve-year-old son, Demoryea Polidore, and her older son's girlfriend, Alicia Jordan, testified to their eyewitness observations of the shooting of the two officers. They all testified that defend-

ant Regis Thomas had the same features and the same body type as the person they observed shoot the officers.

2. *Red 1992 Chevrolet 454 pickup truck.* Based on the testimony of Margaretta Gully and the passengers in her car, it was established that the black male who shot the police officers was driving a red pickup truck. Evidence was presented that on March 9, 1992, Regis Thomas purchased a red 1992 Chevrolet 454 pickup truck and regularly drove the vehicle. Mrs. Gully and the occupants of her car testified that there was "nothing different" between Thomas' red pickup truck depicted in photographs shown to her and the pickup truck driven by the person who shot the officers.

3. *Murder weapon.* A Sig Sauer nine-millimeter pistol was recovered by the police and determined by ballistics tests to be the murder weapon. Keyon Pie, a female friend of defendant Regis Thomas, testified that sometime in February 1993, Thomas came to her house and asked her to hold a gun for him. The next day, pursuant to Thomas' directions, she gave the gun to a man who came to her house to pick up the gun.

4. *Calvin Cooksey.* The person to whom Keyon Pie gave the gun was Calvin Cooksey. He testified that a few days after the murder, Regis Thomas told him that he had shot the two officers. Cooksey agreed to dispose of the murder weapon; he picked up the gun from Keyon Pie at her residence. That evening he sold the gun to Robert Rojas for $260. A few weeks later, he assisted police in the recovery of the gun by purchasing the gun back from Rojas for $350 and turning it over to the police. On the witness stand, Cooksey admitted seven prior felony convictions, including burglary and robbery.

5. *Autopsies.* The cause of death of both officers was ascribed to multiple bullet wounds. This helped corroborate the testimony of

Margaretta Gully and her passengers, who observed the suspect fire multiple times at each officer.

Defense attorney Jay Jaffe attempted to impeach the prosecution witnesses by showing some differences between the statements that they made to investigating officers and the testimony they gave before the jury. However, he was unable to establish any major inconsistencies.

During the defense portion of the case, the defense called witnesses from the crime lab, an officer who testified to prior inconsistent statements of some witnesses, and an expert on eyewitness identification. Defendant Regis Thomas did not testify. The defense did not call any alibi witnesses to testify that Thomas was not at the scene of the shootings.

CLOSING ARGUMENTS AND JURY VERDICT

On April 28, 1995, prosecutor Mark Arnold presented his opening argument to the jury. First, he discussed the Carlos Atkins murder. He argued that the jury should believe Bertrand Dickson despite his seven prior felony convictions since his testimony was amply corroborated by the testimony of Janice Chappell. He then told the jury that the proper verdict for the death of Carlos Atkins was second-degree murder.

> *"However, I think the more proper verdict--the more accurate verdict on the death of Carlos Atkins--is that it's a second-degree murder. It is the unlawful killing of a human being with malice aforethought. I think that is the appropriate verdict.*
>
> *"Could you find that it is a first-degree murder? Yes, you could, but this, I believe, the evidence cries out that Carlos Atkins died as a result of a second-degree murder." (Reporter's trial transcript, page 4072.)*

Prosecutor Arnold then reviewed the evidence of the shootings of Officers Kevin Burrell and James MacDonald and forcefully argued that these were first-degree murders.

> *"This is willful, this is deliberate and premeditated. While there is some question as to whether Carlos Atkins died as a result of a first-degree murder, there should be no question that these two officers died as a result of a first-degree murder. This is a willful, deliberate and pre-meditated murder. Both of these officers, based on everything that we have heard so far, the manner [in] which they were shot, the number of times they were shot and the way that the suspect stood over those two poor uniformed officers posed no threat to that suspect, and they continued to have bullets shot into them." (Reporter's trial transcript, pages 4095-6.)*

The arguments were concluded late on the Friday afternoon of April 28, 1995. Deputy District Attorney Mark Arnold finished his closing argument by summarizing all the evidence against the defendant Regis Thomas and telling the jury:

> *"It is inescapable that the totality of the circumstances – by the totality of the circumstances, as I said before--it is not Alicia Jordan, it is not Mrs. Gully, it is not Keyon Pie, and it is not Deshaunna Cody. It is everything. It's everything." (Reporter's trial transcript, page 4237.)*

The jury was instructed on the law on Monday, May 1, 1995, and began its deliberations. On May 17, 1995, the jury found defendant Regis Thomas guilty of the second-degree murder of Carlos Atkins and the first-degree murders of Officers Kevin Burrell and James MacDonald. The jury found true the special circumstance allegations of multiple murders and murder of a police officer, making the defendant eligible for the death penalty. The same jury would determine whether Thomas should receive a penalty of death or a sentence of life in prison without the possibility of parole.

The penalty phase of the trial began on May 31, 1995.

PENALTY PHASE -- PROSECUTION

In the penalty phase, the prosecution can present evidence in aggravation, such as other criminal acts committed by the defendant. The prosecution can also present witness impact testimony to demonstrate how the death of the victim has affected the lives of friends and relatives.

In aggravation, prosecutor Mark Arnold submitted court records that Regis Thomas had pleaded guilty to charges involving the unlawful possession of a loaded firearm. He also presented testimony from two Housing Authority Police Officers of an incident in February 1990 involving an assault on the officers after a foot pursuit and the recovery of a loaded handgun.

Carlos Atkins' mother testified that after her son's death she no longer went out, and she had been hospitalized for a nervous breakdown. He was a good father to his four children and was attending college to study architecture.

The victim impact testimony of James and Tonia MacDonald, the parents of James MacDonald, was especially heartfelt and anguished; it left many of the courtroom spectators in tears. Their younger son had always wanted to be a police officer. The night that he was shot was his last as a reserve police officer for the City of Compton. He had accepted a full-time position with the San Jose Police Department, which was closer to his parents' home in Santa Rosa. MacDonald's father testified that his son was buried at Memorial Park in Santa Rosa and that he visited the cemetery every day. He thinks about his son constantly, and if he could talk to him one more time he would say, "Come home, Jimmy, and let me trade places with you."

MacDonald's mother testified that her sons Jon and Jimmy were very close. Jon's first child was born three weeks after Jimmy died, so he never got to see his niece. She went to the cemetery twice a day. She testified, "Jimmy was a part of me. I carried him for nine months. That was part of my body that is dead now, and I have said before that I think when Jimmy was ascending into heaven that he reached down, put his hand on my heart, tore a piece out and took it with him." If she could talk to him one more time, she would say, "I pray for Jimmy and Kevin. God is watching over them, and I pray that God will let Jimmy's spirit come just one more time, so I can tell him goodbye, tell him how much I love him and how proud I am of him and I miss him."

Kevin Burrell's parents testified that he had been close to his family and visited them almost every day. His parents lived about eight blocks from the location of the shooting; his mother heard the gunshots. His mother testified that she suffered anxiety attacks since her son's death and sometimes could not leave the house. She was emotionally unable to visit her son's grave at Inglewood Cemetery. If she could talk to Kevin one more time, she stated, "I would tell him . . . how much I loved him and how proud I am of him, and I know he's with the Lord now, but I miss him, you know. It is like part of me gone. I can feel it. I can feel something is gone away from me. Then I get to thinking about him."

Defense attorney Jay Jaffe did not ask questions of any of the parents of the murder victims.

PENALTY PHASE – DEFENSE CASE IN MITIGATION

Family members and friends of the defendant Regis Thomas testified to his early life growing up without a father. He lived with his mother, two brothers, and two sisters. When Thomas was six years old, his mother became addicted to cocaine, and lost her house because of her addiction. Thomas was upset about his mother's cocaine use and often asked her to stop. He would get upset when people used cocaine at the house.

Defendant's wife, Deshaunna Cody, testified that Regis Thomas had been a good husband and good father to their four children. Kawasci Jackson was a former girlfriend and the mother of his son; she testified that he never abused her, and that their son loved his father. Iris Thomas, the defendant's mother, asked the jury not to kill her son, stating, "If you take my son, you may as well take me too."

During cross-examination of some defense witnesses, prosecutor Mark Arnold attempted to show that Thomas had money even though he was not known to have a job. He asked one witness if she knew where Thomas had obtained the money to buy a truck. When Arnold asked the defendant's mother if she knew that her son had paid $18,000 for a truck, the trial court admonished the prosecutor and told him not to pursue this line of questioning.

Arnold asked Kawasci Jackson whether Thomas paid child support for their son. She replied that he did not, although he had given her a total of eighty dollars when she had asked for some money.

VERDICT AND SENTENCING

After argument by the attorneys, Judge Edward Ferns instructed the jury on the law applicable in the penalty phase. The jury deliberated over several days, reaching a verdict that set the penalty for the murders of the officers at death.

On July 17, 1995, Judge Ferns denied the defense motion for a new trial and also denied the defense motion to modify the sentence from death to life imprisonment without the possibility of parole. Judge Ferns then imposed the death sentence on Regis Deon Thomas.

CALIFORNIA SUPREME COURT DECISION

Under California law, every defendant sentenced to death receives an automatic appeal to the California Supreme Court.

On February 23, 2012, the California Supreme Court unanimously affirmed the death sentence of Regis Deon Thomas for the murders of Compton Police Officers Kevin Burrell and James Wayne MacDonald. The decision came nineteen years and one day after the shooting deaths of the two officers.

Chief Justice Tani Cantil-Sakauye wrote the opinion. The main contention on appeal was that the Carlos Atkins murder should have been tried separately from the charges of murder of the two police officers. Justice Cantil-Sakauye wrote that the charges were properly joined because they were all murders; the trial court's denial of the motion to sever was not an abuse of discretion.

Although there are over 700 prisoners on California's death row, only a small number have had their death sentences affirmed by the California Supreme Court. This decision by the California Supreme Court puts Regis Thomas one step closer to the imposition of his death sentence. However, at the time of this writing, no person has been executed under the California death penalty law since 2006.

LESSONS LEARNED

The traffic stop of Regis Thomas took place shortly after 11:00 p.m. on Rosecrans Avenue, a major street in the city of Compton. The area of the stop was well lit and heavily traveled. This may have created a sense of security on the part of Officers Burrell and MacDonald that this was a routine stop that posed no danger to them. They were not aware that Regis Thomas had a history of being in possession of a firearm in his previous contacts with law enforcement.

Normally, a two-officer police car has a numerical and tactical advantage in a traffic stop involving a vehicle with a single occupant. However, the officers must work as a team in coordinating their efforts to maximize officer safety. This is effected by one officer making direct contact with the occupant of the vehicle while the second officer assumes a position at the rear of the vehicle. The officer in contact with the driver should be professional and courteous in the interaction with the driver. The presence of the second officer as the "cover" officer behind the vehicle should be benign and non-confrontational, and the detention should end without incident.

Regis Thomas had a gun in his waistband when his vehicle was pulled over for a traffic violation. He did not want to go to jail, and he decided to shoot the officers if given the opportunity.

During the detention of Regis Thomas, it appears that Officers Burrell and MacDonald were standing in close proximity to him. When Thomas pulled a gun from his waistband, he was able to shoot the officers in one quick motion. By the time the officers learned of Thomas' murderous intent, it was too late. Both officers died with their service revolvers still in their holsters.

The importance of contact and cover officers remaining separated cannot be overemphasized. It is important that the suspect have divided attention. Also, officers need to continually remind themselves that, "There is no such thing as a routine traffic stop."

Officer Kevin Burrell

Date of birth:	May 5, 1963
Date appointed:	July 3, 1988
End of watch:	February 22, 1993

Officer James MacDonald

Date of birth:	November 4, 1968
Date appointed:	June 4, 1991
End of watch:	February 22, 1993

Police car in the rain on Rosecrans Ave. just east of Dwight Ave.

The red 1992 Chevrolet 454 pickup truck driven by Regis Thomas.

The murder weapon: a Sig Sauer nine-millimeter semiautomatic pistol.

Prosecutor Mark Arnold has had a successful professional career in three professions -- first as a deputy sheriff (1975-1985); then as a deputy district attorney (1985-1998); and finally as a superior court judge (1999-Present)

James MacDonald, father of slain officer, on the witness stand

"Come home, Jimmy, let me trade places with you"

Edna Burrell, mother of slain officer, on the witness stand

Clark Burrell, father of slain officer, views family photos while testifying

Regis Deon Thomas

Convicted of murders of Carlos Adkins, Officer Kevin Burrell, and Officer James MacDonald

Sentenced to death

CHAPTER FOUR

Officer Martin Ganz

Manhattan Beach Police Department

"Traffic Stop Risk"

December 27, 1993

OFFICER MARTIN GANZ
MANHATTAN BEACH POLICE DEPARTMENT

MARTIN GANZ WAS BORN ON JULY 13, 1964. He was the only male sibling in the family; he had seven sisters. From the time he was twelve years old, he wanted to be a police officer. As a young teenager, he was an Explorer for the Garden Grove Police Department. After he graduated from high school, he joined the Marines, so he could receive training as a military police officer.

In 1988, Ganz was hired by the Manhattan Beach Police Department in a civilian position involving community outreach. He became a sworn police officer in 1989, first assigned to motorcycle duty and then as a uniformed police officer in a marked police vehicle. He was a respected and popular officer who genuinely enjoyed serving the public as a police officer.

Officer Ganz was very close to his sisters, often providing them with emotional and financial support. He was especially close to his sister, Rachel Ganz-Williams, a single mother who lived in Florida with her two children. Her twelve-year-old son, Don Ganz, was Martin Ganz's nephew and godson. During December 1993, Don Ganz was in Los Angeles visiting from Florida on a Christmas vacation.

Officer Ganz was engaged to marry Pamela Ham. She had accepted his proposal of marriage in early December 1993. He had purchased a home and was remodeling it in anticipation of the marriage.

Officer Ganz worked on Christmas Eve in December 1993 so that other officers in the Manhattan Beach Police Department could spend time with their families. After his shift was over, he celebrated Christmas morning at the home of one of his sisters and her children.

Two days later, Officer Martin Ganz would be the first officer from the Manhattan Beach Police Department to die in the line of duty.

DECEMBER 27, 1993

On December 27, 1993, Martin Ganz spent the day with his twelve-year-old nephew and godson Don Ganz. They first went to Home Depot and then had lunch at Arby's. Later that day, they attended a 3:00 p.m. briefing at the Manhattan Beach Police Station, where Officer Ganz changed into his police uniform. Officer Ganz then went on patrol duty in a marked police vehicle, accompanied by Don, in a department-sanctioned "ride along."

Officer Ganz showed Don how to use the police radio should anything happen. They spent the rest of the afternoon and the evening on patrol, with Officer Ganz writing tickets for about ten of the fifteen traffic violators who were pulled over. At one point, Officer Ganz drove to the Manhattan Beach Pier where he asked a passer-by to take a photograph of him and his nephew with the glowing sunset in the background.

At 11:00 p.m., toward the end of his watch, Officer Ganz observed a small gray or silver car stopped for a red light on Sepulveda Boulevard. The car was stopped past the limit line of the crosswalk, partially blocking the intersection. Officer Ganz activated the patrol vehicle's spotlight and shined it on the driver, the sole occupant of the vehicle. He used his loudspeaker to order the driver to back up. The driver backed his car a short distance, but it remained over the limit line. When the traffic light at the intersection changed, the car turned into the parking lot of the Manhattan Village parking mall. Officer Ganz followed the car and pulled it over next to a Bank of America branch in the mall. He stopped his patrol vehicle about three or four feet behind the car. He did not report over the air the location of the stop or the license plate of the detained vehicle. Officer Ganz told Don, "I'll be right back." He got out of the police vehicle and walked to the driver's side window of the small gray or silver car. Jennifer La Fond worked at one of the stores in the mall; she drove by as Officer Ganz walked toward the car.

THE DEATH OF OFFICER MARTIN GANZ

Officer Ganz briefly spoke to the driver of the car. The driver leaned toward the passenger side of his car as if retrieving something from the glove compartment or the passenger seat. Witnesses at the mall, including Don Ganz and Jennifer La Fond, then heard a loud "pop" as if a gun were being fired. Officer Ganz fell back as if he had been struck by a bullet and moved quickly toward the rear of the police vehicle in a crouched position. The occupant of the small gray or silver car exited his car and followed approximately six to twelve feet behind the officer. As Officer Ganz retreated to the rear of the police vehicle, the gunman fired a second shot into the officer's back. Officer Ganz either fell or dove behind the police vehicle. The gunman then took a combat stance by holding his gun with both hands and fired a final shot into the officer's head. The gunman lingered for a few moments at the scene before returning to his car and driving off.

Upon seeing his uncle being shot, Don Ganz ducked on the floor of the police vehicle and curled into a ball. He heard his uncle's footsteps running along the driver's side of the police vehicle. He looked up and saw the gunman near the rear of the police car fire a second shot with fire coming from the barrel of the gun. The gunman then held the gun with both hands and fired a third shot. Don could hear a flashlight hit the ground and then his uncle hit the ground.

Hearing no more shots, Don lifted his head again and saw the gunman standing in front of him, pointing the gun at him through the windshield. The terrified boy ducked again and heard the gunman's car drive off. Don then grabbed the police radio and screamed for help. He ran to his uncle who was lying face down behind the police vehicle in a pool of blood. Officer Ganz was making gurgling noises and struggling to breathe. A woman took the hysterical boy to the curb while several bystanders came to Officer Ganz's assistance. One placed his head in her lap to remove him from the puddle of blood that was choking him. Another used the police radio to call for help.

Just after 11:00 p.m., the Communications Division of the Manhattan Beach Police Department heard the panicked and anguished screams of twelve-year-old Don Ganz over the police radio. Moments later another voice came on over the radio crying out, "Someone's been shot, an officer's been shot . . . He's dying. He needs help!"

Officers in the field responded immediately to radio broadcasts of the shooting. One officer who responded was Manhattan Beach Police Officer Neal O'Gilvey, one of Ganz's closest friends. He rode in the back of an ambulance with Officer Ganz on the way to Los Angeles County Harbor-UCLA Medical Center. He held the mortally wounded officer's hand and screamed at him to keep fighting. Ganz's grip on Officer O'Gilvey's hand gradually weakened. Officer Martin Ganz died from his injuries in the hospital's emergency room.

CRIME SCENE INVESTIGATION

The Los Angeles County Sheriff's Department has an excellent Homicide Bureau of experienced detectives who investigate murders in smaller cities in the county where police departments do not have the manpower or resources to conduct their own homicide investigations. In particular, the murder of a law enforcement officer demands that the best available resources and expertise are deployed in the investigation. The Sheriff's Homicide Bureau handled the investigation into the death of Manhattan Beach Police Officer Martin Ganz.

At approximately 1:00 in the morning of December 28, 1993, Detective Joseph Raffa of the Sheriff's Homicide Bureau arrived at the crime scene and handled the crime scene investigation. He recovered three spent shell casings fired from a .380 automatic; two were near the front of the police vehicle and the other was next to the driver's side. He also obtained videotapes from the security camera systems of two nearby banks. These videotapes were delivered to an institute affiliated with the National Institute of Justice. After analyzing the videotapes, the Institute advised

Sheriff's investigators that the suspect was diving a Daihatsu Charade hatchback with damage to the right front side. However, the license plate information on the vehicle could not be determined from the videotapes. There were approximately eight thousand vehicles of this make and model registered in California at that time, which made connecting the suspect vehicle to a particular individual virtually impossible

Numerous witnesses, including Donald Ganz and Jennifer La Fond, were taken to the police station where they were interviewed. They described various aspects of the shooter, his vehicle, and the circumstances of the shooting.

AUTOPSY

On December 28, 1993, an autopsy was performed on the body of Officer Martin Ganz by Solomon Riley, M.D., a deputy medical examiner for the Los Angeles County Coroner's Office. Officer Ganz had sustained two gunshot wounds. One bullet entered the left side of his face just below the eye, fractured the orbital bone, grazed the brain, and lodged beneath the right ear. In Dr. Riley's opinion, this was the gunshot wound that caused the death of Officer Ganz. Such a wound would have rendered the officer unconscious in a matter of seconds and unable to run a distance of more than a few feet. The second gunshot wound entered the right side of Ganz's upper chest, passed through the chest wall, broke the bone in his upper right arm, and exited through the back of his right arm. In addition, Officer Ganz had a contusion on his back that was consistent with being shot in the back while wearing a bulletproof vest.

From eyewitness accounts and the coroner's findings, detectives surmised that Officer Ganz was first shot in the upper chest above his bulletproof vest while at the suspect's vehicle. With the bone in his right arm broken, he was unable to draw his service revolver and retreated to the rear of his police vehicle. The suspect then fired a second shot into the officer's back that lodged in his bulletproof vest. The suspect then fired the fatal shot into the face of the officer.

PRELIMINARY INVESTIGATION

Detectives Delores Perales and Clemente Bonilla were the lead investigators of the Compton Homicide Task Force investigating the murder of Officer Martin Ganz. Despite the presence of numerous eyewitnesses to the crime and the existence of two videotapes, investigators were unable to identify the person responsible for the murder. At one time there were about one hundred law enforcement personnel, mostly from South Bay law enforcement agencies, working on the case.

The Sheriff's Department established a hotline to receive tips from the public concerning the murder of Officer Ganz. There were about two thousand clues that law enforcement received from the public and other sources. These clues were numbered and categorized. Officers were then given the more promising clues and leads, and they later reported to Detectives Perales and Bonilla the results of their follow-up investigations.

On January 20, 1994, Clue 1270 was received, which implicated Roger Hoan Brady to the murder of Officer Ganz. Investigators learned that Brady was on federal parole for bank robbery. They contacted his parole officer, advised him of the investigation, and received his authority to conduct a parole search of Brady, if one would be necessary. They determined that the 28-year old Brady lived with his parents and that a 1988 Daihatsu Charade was registered in his father's name. He bore a resemblance to a composite drawing of the murder suspect. Brady became a prime target for further investigation.

Two officers in the Task Force were assigned to investigate Roger Brady. Initially they conducted a brief surveillance and determined that he worked at a McDonald's restaurant. The officers then went to the condominium where Brady lived with his parents. They conducted a parole search which was limited by law to a search of his bedroom and common areas of the residence.

They were looking for a .380 magnum semi-automatic handgun, but they did not find anything of evidentiary value. They also searched the 1988 Daihatsu Charade parked nearby. It had damage to its right side and was registered to Brady's father. The officers believed that there was insufficient evidence to connect Brady to the murder of Officer Ganz, and no arrest was made.

Roger Brady remained a viable suspect, and his photograph was included in a photo book of suspects maintained by investigators. On a couple of occasions, Detectives Perales and Bonilla flew to Florida where Don Ganz was living to show him the murder book. However, he did not identify anyone as the shooter. Jennifer La Fond also failed to identify anyone when she examined the photo book. The use of the photo book may have been hampered by the large number of photographs and the age or quality of some of them.

RELOCATION OF ROGER BRADY

The visit by the officers to the condominium alerted Roger Brady that he was a suspect in the murder of Officer Ganz. Brady's parents had lived in the Los Angeles area since the mid-1970s, but the entire Brady family left California and relocated to the state of Washington. By April 1994, Roger Brady and his parents were residing at 4701 N.E. 72nd Avenue, Apartment X278, Vancouver, Washington. Brady was still on federal parole, and he notified his parole officer of his change of address. Brady's father, Philip Brady, registered the 1988 Daihatsu Charade with the Washington Motor Vehicle Department and obtained license plate number 753 FSA for the vehicle.

AUGUST 3, 1994 | ROBBERY-HOMICIDE IN OREGON

On August 3, 1994, at about 10:20 p.m., Roger Huan Brady entered a Safeway store on Cornell Road in Portland, Oregon. He was wearing a long beige coat with a hood and a dark blue ski mask that partially covered his face. He approached a clerk inside the store, pulled out a semi-automatic pistol, and told the clerk to open the cash drawer and back away. Brady then took money from the drawer and ran from the store. As he was running, he rounded the corner where a fifty-five-year-old woman named Catalina Correa turned and faced him. Mrs. Correa had just left the store and had groceries in her arms. Brady fired two shots at Mrs. Correa striking her in the neck and in the chest. She died at the scene. Two .380 cartridges were recovered near her body.

Brett Ferguson was driving into the Safeway store parking lot and saw a person wearing a tan coat and a hood approach a woman standing on the sidewalk carrying some groceries. The person pulled out a gun and fired two or three shots at the woman. She fell to the ground. The shooter then entered a vehicle and slowly drove out of the parking lot without its lights on. It was followed by a white van. Ferguson went to the female victim, checked for a pulse, and attempted to communicate with her. However, she was unresponsive and appeared to be deceased.

Andrew Dickson was driving his white Toyota van into the parking lot of the Safeway store when he saw a person shoot a gun and a woman fall to the sidewalk. The shooter entered a Daihatsu vehicle and backed up to Dickson's car before driving off. Dickson observed that the suspect's vehicle had Washington license plate 753 FSA, which he committed to memory. He saw that other people were running to attend the victim, so he decided to follow the suspect's vehicle.

Dickson followed the vehicle for two or three blocks before it came to a stop. He then stopped his vehicle approximately fifty yards behind the suspect's vehicle. Apparently, the suspect knew he was being followed, since he exited his car and fired several shots from a rifle at Dickson's white Toyota van. Three shots struck the Toyota van with one shot breaking the windshield. Dickson ducked behind the windshield, put the gear into reverse, and quickly backed away from the location. The suspect then re-entered his vehicle and drove off.

Police investigators obtained the vehicle plate information from Andrew Dickson. A check with the Motor Vehicle Department determined that the registration information for Washington license plate 753 FSA was for a 1988 Daihatsu registered to Philip Brady at 4701 N.E. 72nd Avenue, Apartment X278, Vancouver, Washington.

ROBBERY-MURDER (OREGON) INVESTIGATION

Vancouver Police Department officers went to the Brentwood Apartments at 4701 N.E. 72nd Avenue and located a 1988 gray Daihatsu license number 753 FSA in the apartment complex parking lot. The engine compartment was warm to the touch. Officers began a constant surveillance of the vehicle and of Apartment 278 of building X at the apartment complex.

On August 4, 1994, at 7:00 a.m., investigating officers obtained a search warrant authorizing the search of the 1988 Daihatsu and of Apartment 278 in the apartment complex. The search warrant was executed later that morning. Nothing of evidentiary value was found inside the vehicle. The search warrant for Apartment 278 was executed at approximately 8:30 a.m. Roger Huan Brady was inside the apartment where he lived with his parents Philip and Diep Brady. Roger Brady was placed under arrest without incident. A search of the apartment resulted in the recovery of two wigs, an assault rifle, and ammunition for that rifle. Officers conducting the search observed a locked security box in the cupboard underneath the sink of the master bedroom used by Philip and Diep Brady. Mr. Brady told the officers that the security box belonged to his son, Roger, and that he did not know Roger was keeping it under the sink.

The officers seized the security box and obtained another search warrant to unlock and search the box. The box contained a semi-automatic .380 caliber handgun, two ammunition magazines, a box of .380 caliber ammunition, an envelope, two pairs of gloves, and a ski mask. Ballistics tests determined that Catalina Correa had been shot with Brady's .380 caliber pistol, and Andrew Dickson had been shot at by Brady's assault rifle.

ROGER HUAN BRADY

Roger Huan Brady was born in Vietnam on October 31, 1965, to a Vietnamese mother and an American father. His father, Philip Brady, was a young United States Marine who spoke Vietnamese and served as an adviser to South Vietnamese troops. His mother, Diep, had two brothers in the South Vietnamese Army. One of her brothers was killed in battle, and Philip contacted Diep so she could retrieve her brother's belongings. They began to date, and she became pregnant with their child.

Philip was transferred to the United States and was not present when Roger Huan Brady was born. (The middle name "Huan" was in honor of Diep's slain brother.) Philip returned to Vietnam when his son was eight months old. Philip, Diep, and Roger lived in security compounds in Vietnam and Cambodia while the war waged all around them. Roger was the only child in those compounds and on several occasions observed soldiers being killed.

When Roger was age three-and-a-half, the family moved to New York when Philip was offered a job as a journalist. However, the family moved back to Vietnam where Philip became a journalist for NBC. While in Vietnam, Philip suffered from flashbacks and extensively used drugs and alcohol. He was physically abusive to Diep and Roger.

Eventually the family returned to the United States and settled in the Southern California area. Around 1977, the family bought a home in a remote area in Topanga, California. Philip cultivated marijuana, and Roger helped attend to the plants. By the age of thirteen, Roger was using marijuana. Philip continued his physical abuse toward Roger and Diep.

Roger graduated from high school and wanted to join the military, but Philip told him that he was too weak. Instead, Roger attended a local community college.

From August to October 1989, Roger Brady robbed six banks in the Los Angeles area and attempted to commit two additional bank robberies. On each occasion, he demanded money from a teller, and, on some occasions, he displayed a firearm tucked in his waistband. He was arrested on October 12, 1989, after a police pursuit following the last of these bank robberies. He was in possession of a BB gun and intimated to the arresting officer that he would have shot it out with police. Next time, he said, he would not be armed with just a BB gun.

Brady was charged in federal court with six counts of bank robbery. He was sentenced to federal prison after pleading guilty to two counts of bank robbery. He served approximately three years in custody before his release on October 1, 1992. The terms of his supervised release prohibited him from possessing firearms.

From October to December 1993, Roger Brady robbed five supermarkets in the Los Angeles area. During the robberies, he wore an obviously fake wig, displayed or brandished a gun, and demanded money. On December 27, 1993, the date of the murder of Officer Martin Ganz, Brady was still on supervised release. If Officer Ganz had recovered the .380 semiautomatic in his possession, Brady would have been returned to federal prison. Brady did not commit any additional robberies in the Los Angeles area after the murder of Officer Ganz.

From April to July 1994, Roger Brady robbed five supermarkets and a pharmacy near the Washington-Oregon border. On these occasions, he usually wore a long coat and a ski mask that covered most of his face. He demanded money (and certain drugs during the pharmacy robbery) and displayed or brandished a firearm that he carried in his waistband.

Roger Huan Brady's lengthy crime spree ended with his arrest on August 4, 1994.

AUGUST 1994 – POST ARREST EVENTS

A records check of Roger Brady by Oregon authorities after his arrest disclosed that he was on federal parole for bank robbery. Brady's parole officer was contacted and notified of Brady's arrest and the recovery of a .380 caliber handgun. The parole officer in turn contacted the investigating officers on the Ganz murder and told them of Brady's arrest in Washington and the recovery of the handgun. Detectives Perales and Bonilla quickly moved to connect Brady to the murder of Officer Martin Ganz.

- The detectives flew to Oregon with Sheriff's ballistic expert Dwight Van Horne who had possession of the bullets recovered from Officer Ganz's vest and body. He compared the bullets to the .380 caliber handgun and concluded that they had been fired from Brady's firearm.
- Brady's 1988 Daihatsu vehicle was identical in appearance to the car depicted on the bank's videotapes, including the damage to the right front side.
- Jennifer La Fond had failed to identify Brady in May 1994 when she examined the photo book with his photograph. However, she identified Brady as the shooter on August 13, 1994, when she observed him in person at a lineup in Oregon.
- Donald Ganz failed to identify Brady when he examined the photo book. However, at the live lineup in Oregon on August 13, 1994, he identified Brady as the shooter.

The Los Angeles County District Attorney's Office filed murder charges against Roger Brady on August 24, 1994. Extradition proceedings to bring Brady from Oregon to Los Angeles were delayed because the Oregon authorities wanted first to prosecute Brady for crimes committed in Oregon. Brady was charged in Oregon with the murder of Catalina Correa, attempted aggravated murder of Andrew Dickson, and the robbery of the Safeway store. On November 2, 1995, an Oregon jury convicted him of these charges. Although the prosecution in Oregon sought the death penalty, the jury imposed a sentence of life in prison without parole.

After his conviction in Oregon, Brady was extradited to Los Angeles and booked into the Los Angeles County Jail on August 1, 1996, to face criminal charges for the murder of Officer Martin Ganz.

Below is a summary of the criminal charges in Los Angeles against Roger Hoan Brady and the principal parties in the case.

PEOPLE v. ROGER HUAN BRADY
Case YA020910

JUDGE:	The Honorable Stephen E. O'Neill
PROSECUTOR:	Barbara Turner, Deputy District Attorney
DEFENSE ATTORNEY:	Regina Laughney, Deputy Public Defender
CHARGES:	Murder in the First Degree

- Special Circumstance of Murder Committed Against a Peace Officer Engaged in Performance of His Duties
- Special Circumstance of Murder for the Purpose of Avoiding or Preventing a Lawful Arrest
- Special Circumstance That Defendant Has Previously Been Convicted of Murder

LOCATION:	Los Angeles Superior Court Torrance Courthouse
DATES OF TRIAL:	October 14, 1998 to December 16, 1998

BARBARA TURNER, DEPUTY DISTRICT ATTORNEY

Barbara Turner became a Deputy District Attorney in 1985 and had a remarkable career as a prosecutor. When she joined the District Attorney's Office, it was a male-dominated organization. John Van de Kamp, the District Attorney, changed the demographics of the office by hiring large numbers of women and placing them in positions of authority throughout the office. Turner was one of many female hires who proved the wisdom of Van de Kamp's policy. She was a skillful trial lawyer who was assigned to two of the premier trial units in the District Attorney's Office: first, the Hardcore Gang Division prosecuting murder cases against gang members and, later, the Crimes Against Police Officers Section (CAPOS) prosecuting defendants who murdered or committed serious assaults against members of law enforcement. It was as a member of CAPOS that she prosecuted Roger Huan Brady for the murder of Officer Martin Ganz.

Barbara Turner later served four years as the Assistant Head Deputy in the Major Narcotics Division. She became an expert in the area of wiretaps and helped make major revisions in the California wiretap statute in 2001 and 2002. She lectured to law enforcement groups on how to obtain a valid wiretap under the California statute and assisted many officers in the preparation of legal wiretaps. In 2004, she was honored as the Prosecutor of the Year by the California Narcotic Officers Association.

She later spent six years as the Assistant Head Deputy of the Airport Branch Office and one year as the Deputy-in-Charge of the Environmental Law Section. She retired in 2014, after twenty-nine years of public service.

PEOPLE v. ROGER HUAN BRADY

The jury trial in the case of People v. Roger Huan Brady began in the Torrance courtroom of Judge Stephen O'Neill on October 14, 1998. Over 100 potential jurors filled the courtroom as jury selection began to select a panel to decide the fate of the man charged with the murder of Manhattan Beach police officer Martin Ganz on December 27, 1993, nearly five years prior. Since the prosecution was seeking the death penalty, prospective jurors were questioned about their views on the death penalty.

A jury was selected, and the attorneys made their opening statements on Monday, October 26, 1998. Prosecutor Barbara Turner began her opening statement in dramatic fashion by playing the chilling tape of twelve-year-old Don Ganz screaming into the police radio that his uncle had been shot. After playing the tape, Turner spoke for just seven minutes in briefly describing her case. In a short five-minute opening statement, Deputy Public Defender Regina Laughney questioned the identifications of the two witnesses who identified her client as the killer and suggested that the wrong person was being prosecuted.

Don Ganz took the witness stand the following day. He was now seventeen-years-old and looked far different from the twelve-year-old boy who had witnessed his uncle's murder almost five years before. He was much taller and sported a thin mustache. He was wearing a black suit and a black-and-white tie bearing a five-pointed star. There were at least ten members of his family and other relatives in the courtroom to support him.

After taking the witness stand, Don Ganz began to cry. After about thirty seconds, he composed himself and told the judge, "I'm all right. I'm all right." Under the gentle but focused questioning of Deputy District Attorney Barbara Turner, Don Ganz spent the next two-and-a-half to three hours describing the events of December 27, 1993, in chilling and dramatic fashion. He made a courtroom identification of the defendant, Roger Brady, as the person who shot his uncle. Defense attorney Regina Laughney conducted a brief cross-examination as Don Ganz spent less than one day on the witness stand.

Over seven court days, prosecutor Turner presented testimony that included eyewitness identifications of Brady as the killer by Don Ganz and Jennifer La Fond. Other evidence linked Brady's .380 semiautomatic and his 1988 Daihatsu to the killing. Turner concluded the presentation of her case-in-chief on November 5, 1998.

Roger Brady did not testify in his defense. Defense Attorney Laughney presented a short defense that included impeaching the eyewitnesses with prior inconsistent statements.

The evidentiary portion of the trial ended abruptly, and the attorneys presented their closing arguments to the jury on Monday, November 9, 1998. The jury began deliberating on November 10, 1998. On November 12, the jury found Roger Brady guilty of first-degree murder with two special circumstances of murder of a police officer and murder to prevent or avoid a lawful arrest. The special circumstance findings made Brady eligible for the death penalty. The same jury that had decided his guilt would determine whether he should serve a life sentence without parole or receive the death penalty.

PRIOR OREGON MURDER CONVICTION

On Friday, November 13, 1998, Deputy District Attorney Barbara Turner presented documentary evidence from Oregon to establish that Roger Brady had been convicted on November 2, 1995, of robbery, attempted murder, and aggravated murder in Washington County Circuit Court in Hillsboro, Oregon. The jury deliberated only 30 minutes to find that Brady had committed these crimes. This prior murder conviction was a third special circumstance making Brady eligible for the death penalty.

This was the first time that the jurors were made aware of Roger Brady's murder conviction in Oregon. This special circumstance allegation—having a prior murder conviction—was deemed so prejudicial that the judge and the attorneys agreed that evidence of this murder could only be presented to the jury if Brady was convicted of the first-degree murder of Officer Ganz.

PENALTY PHASE

On Monday, November 16, 1998, the penalty phase began in the case of People v. Roger Huan Brady.

Under the California death penalty statute, the prosecution at the penalty phase can introduce (a) prior criminal activity of the defendant, and (b) victim impact testimony. The United States Supreme Court has ruled that in determining sentence, a jury may consider the circumstances of the crime—including the immediate injurious impact—as an aggravating factor. *Payne v. Tennessee* (1991) 501 U.S. 808. Deputy District Attorney Barbara Turner decided to introduce evidence during the penalty phase that would test statutes and case law in this area to their fullest extent.

PROSECUTION EVIDENCE

Over the course of twelve days, more than sixty witnesses testified during the prosecution case in aggravation at the penalty phase. They included many of the victims of the robberies of banks and stores committed over the years by the defendant. Details of the murder of Catalina Correa in Oregon were introduced. Members of Ganz's family, police officers, and the woman he was engaged to marry each testified to the impact that the death of Martin Ganz had on their lives.

The prosecution introduced a six-minute tape of Officer Ganz's funeral. It depicted Officer Ganz's casket being taken from the church to his gravesite with hundreds of uniformed police officers in attendance. Don Ganz could be seen crying and being comforted by members of his family. Martin Ganz's mother was observed too distraught to get out of her vehicle while at the gravesite.

A four-minute videotape was played for the jury which depicted Officer Ganz celebrating Christmas with members of his family, two days before his death. It consisted primarily of Officer Ganz giving presents to one of his sisters and some of his young nephews and nieces, who excitedly opened the gifts.

One person who did not testify at the penalty phase was Don Ganz. He had returned to his home in Florida after testifying in the guilt phase and was expected to be a witness at the penalty phase. However, Don's mother testified that her son did not testify at the penalty phase because he "just couldn't do it."

One of Martin Ganz's sisters testified that their mother "gave up on life" and died six months after her son's murder.

DEFENSE EVIDENCE

Deputy Public Defender Regina Laughney called Roger Brady's mother and sister to describe his chaotic childhood while growing up in Vietnam. They testified that Brady's father was physically abusive to his son and contributed to Roger's addiction to crack cocaine. Laughney also called a neuropsychologist who examined Brady and concluded that he functioned well in a controlled setting such as a prison and posed no danger to anyone if allowed to remain in prison the rest of his life.

On December 16, 1998, after deliberating less than four hours, the jury recommended that Roger Huan Brady be put to death for the murder of Manhattan Beach police officer Martin Ganz.

CALIFORNIA SUPREME COURT DECISION

In California, every defendant who is sentenced to death has an automatic appeal to the California Supreme Court. The Court issued its opinion on Brady's appeal on August 9, 2010, which appears at *People* v. *Roger Huan Brady* (2010) 50 Cal. 4th 547 of the official judicial reports.

Brady's first-degree murder conviction and death penalty sentence were affirmed in a unanimous decision by the seven-member court. The Court found sufficient evidence to support Brady's conviction for first-degree murder. The Court also found no error in the extensive victim im-pact testimony introduced by the prosecution during the penalty phase of the case.

LESSONS LEARNED

A patrol officer working a one-officer police car is especially vulnerable if the driver of a detained vehicle has an intent to shoot the officer. The officer is aware that the driver has committed a traffic violation. He does not know whether the driver may be armed, on parole, a wanted fugitive, or may have just committed a crime.

It would be a public relations disaster for officers to draw their weapons whenever they make a traffic stop. Officer Ganz made what he believed was a routine traffic stop, not knowing that the driver was on parole for robbery and armed with a handgun. As he approached the driver's side of the vehicle, he was shot and disabled. He tried to get away, but he was chased by the suspect and summarily executed at the rear of his police vehicle.

It is generally safer for a lone officer to approach the stopped vehicle on the passenger side. Most people are right handed, and it would be more difficult, and more time consuming for the suspect to turn and shoot the officer if the officer were on the passenger side. In addition, when allowing suspect drivers (or passengers) to reach into hidden areas, like the glove compartment, they should be instructed to move slowly. It is essential that the officer be keenly aware of the person's movements. Finally, it is basic when conducting a traffic stop for the officer to radio in the location and the license number of the vehicle.

Investigation of the murder of Officer Ganz revealed that it was common practice in the agency in those days to communicate the traffic stop location and related information only after the fact. When Officer Ganz's nephew made the broadcast for help when Ganz was shot, responding units were initially dispatched to his previously reported location. This is indicative of a mind-set that there is such a thing as a "routine traffic stop." There is not, and officers must never allow themselves to fall into that trap.

When the driver of a vehicle for a traffic stop pulls a gun on a patrol officer working a one-officer police car, it is the driver of the detained vehicle who invariably prevails. In most circumstances, the officer does not have time to unholster his sidearm before he is shot. The officer's best (and perhaps only) chance of avoiding serious injury is taking evasive action and moving quickly from the driver's side of the vehicle when an occupant produces a gun.

Two-officer police vehicles should be the norm, if officers will be stopping vehicles for traffic violations. Decreasing the number of citations issued by a police agency is a small price to pay for using two-officer vehicles, which greatly promote officer safety.

As an additional issue to think about when approaching vehicles, conducting building searches, and performing other high-risk activities, many officers (especially at night and in tougher parts of town) "bootleg" their handguns (i.e., surreptitiously draw and hide it behind their thigh as they make their cautious approach) because they think they can react faster if a sudden threat emerges. However, research by the Force Science Research Center disproves this notion. It actually takes much more time (nine-tenths of a second versus less than one-third of a second) to come up on target and fire from the bootleg position than from the position of hand-on-gun in an unsnapped holster. The bootleg position requires a longer physical movement, and officers are much more experienced at rapidly drawing and firing from the holster than the bootleg. An advantage of the bootleg position is that it tends to be "low-profile" to the suspect and any witnesses compared to an officer obviously having his/her hand on the gun, ready to draw it. But the slower speed of the bootleg draw is a distinct disadvantage. This requires officers to consider the trade-off between the potential benefit of the low-profile action versus the need for a speedy reaction time.

Officer Martin Ganz

Date of birth: July 13, 1964
Year of assignment: 1989
End of watch: December 27, 1993

Memorial at Bank of America   **Memorial at Live Oak Park**

Martin Ganz with nephew Don standing next to him and other family members

27 December 1993

a   b

c   Bank of America   d

e

First Interstate Bank

Surveillance camera photos of vehicle stop

Officer Ganz' patrol car at scene of shooting

**Photograph of 12-year-old Don Ganz taken at
police station after shooting of Officer Martin Ganz**

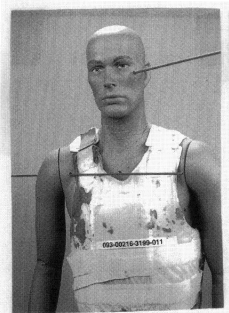
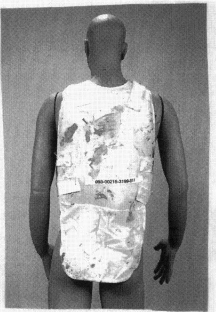

Mannequin showing the trajectory of the two bullets that entered the body of Officer Ganz. A third bullet shot into the officer's back lodged in his bulletproof vest.

August 3, 1994 Robbery - Homicide in Oregon

Roger Hoan Brady robs this Safeway store...

Shoots and kills Catalina Correa outside store...

Drives off in this 1988 Daihatsu...

And is later arrested at his residence.

A locked security box in the cupboard underneath the sink in bathroom of the master bedroom used by Brady's parents contained the .380 semi-automatic handgun used to kill Officer Ganz

December 16, 1998. Roger Hoan Brady responds to jury's death penalty verdict

CHAPTER FIVE

Officer Daniel Timothy Fraembs

Pomona Police Department

"Always Think, 'Backup'"

May 11, 1996

THE MURDER OF OFFICER DANIEL TIMOTHY FRAEMBS

AT APPROXIMATELY 1:30 A.M. ON SATURDAY, MAY 11, 1996, Ronald Mendoza, Joseph Cesena, and Johanna Flores were walking in the 500 block of Humane Way near Mission Boulevard in Pomona, California. This was an industrial area with little vehicular traffic during the nighttime hours. Mendoza and Cesena were members of the "Happy Town" gang in Pomona. Mendoza was on parole and was carrying a pager and a .45 caliber handgun. Flores was involved in a relationship with Mendoza.

Officer Daniel Timothy Fraembs of the Pomona Police Department was in police uniform driving a one-man police car. He observed the three individuals walking late at night in this isolated industrial area and decided to investigate. He stopped the police car near the three individuals and exited the vehicle without reporting his location over the police radio or requesting a backup. Officer Fraembs began a pat-down search of Cesena while Mendoza and Flores stood nearby. Mendoza suddenly produced a gun and fired a shot at Officer Fraembs, striking him in the face. Officer Fraembs fell to the ground, fatally wounded.

After Officer Fraembs was shot, Mendoza and Flores ran from the scene of the shooting to their respective residences. Cesena hid in some bushes nearby.

CRIME SCENE INVESTIGATION

On May 11, 1996 at approximately 1:35 a.m., an unknown citizen driving in the 2100 block of Humane Way saw Officer Fraembs's marked police car parked in the street with the driver's door open. Officer Fraembs in full uniform was lying in the street. The citizen went to a pay phone and called the Pomona Police Department and notified them that a police officer was down at the location.

The call was received at 1:37 a.m. Immediately, assisting police units responded to the scene. Officer Fraembs was lying on his back approximately eight feet from the open patrol car door on the driver's side. His service weapon was unsnapped but holstered. There was a bullet wound on his face. An expended Remington .45 caliber shell casing was located on the roadway approximately eight feet from the officer's body. It was later determined that the bullet entered Officer Fraembs's face by his nose and exited through the back of his head. An expended .45 caliber projectile was later found across the street from the body of the slain officer.

The Los Angeles County Sheriff's Department was the agency that was in charge of conducting the investigation into the death of Pomona Officer Daniel Fraembs. They had the resources and experienced personnel to conduct a major investigation that a smaller agency such as the Pomona Police Department would be unable to perform as well.

An extremely large perimeter was set up, and K-9 handlers from different police agencies of the surrounding cities were called to assist in the search. Over twenty K-9 handlers responded to this request for assistance to search the perimeter.

One of the K-9 handlers who came to the scene of the murder was West Covina Police Officer Brad Smith and his police dog, Rocco. Approximately 100 feet north of Officer Fraembs's body was a vacant and abandoned city incinerator. It was surrounded by overgrown bushes and enclosed by a chain link fence. At approximately 8:00 a.m., Officer Smith and his police dog located Joseph Cesena hiding in the bushes. Cesena was confronted by Rocco, emerged from the bushes, and was arrested.

A pager was located on the sidewalk of Humane Way approximately seventy yards south of Officer Fraembs's body. The pager indicated that it had come from "J and J King of Beepers." The display window on the pager revealed that several pages with phone numbers were stored in the memory. One of the stored numbers was 595-4092 (later determined to be the phone number at Joseph Cesena's residence). A search warrant executed later that day for the company's subscriber records disclosed that the pager had been sold to Ronald Mendoza with an address of 1872 Grier Street, Pomona.

On May 11, at approximately 7:00 p.m., investigators went to 1872 Grier Street, Pomona, the residence where Ronald Mendoza was residing with his mother and stepfather Harry Lukons. Mendoza was not at the residence at that time. Lukons gave consent to the investigators to search the location. One of the investigators found a camera case at the top of a trash can in the back yard. Inside the camera case were seventeen Remington .45 caliber bullets. It was noted that these bullets were the same brand and caliber as the expended casing found near the body of Officer Fraembs.

INTERVIEWS

Several persons were interviewed at the Walnut Sheriff's Station on the date of May 11, 1996, including the following individuals:

Joseph Cesena a.k.a. "Sparky," eighteen-year-old, Hispanic male

Cesena was arrested near the murder scene hiding in the bushes by an abandoned city incinerator. At Walnut Sheriff's Station several investigators interviewed Cesena, but he was reluctant to talk with them. Finally, he was interviewed by Pomona Police Department Detective Collins, with whom Cesena had a number of previous contacts. Eventually he admitted that he was walking with two other people when a police car appeared, and one of the two persons shot the officer. Cesena refused to say where he was when the shot was fired, and he refused to identify the two persons who were with him. He said that he could not tell because the gang would kill him.

There was insufficient evidence to charge Cesena with a crime, but he remained in custody for several weeks on an outstanding juvenile warrant.

Ronald Bruce Mendoza a.k.a. "Boxer," twenty-two-year-old, Hispanic male

Investigators wanted to interview Ronald Mendoza because a pager that he had purchased was found near the crime scene. Mendoza voluntarily came to the Walnut Sheriff's Station on the evening of May 11, where he was questioned by Sheriff's Department Homicide Investigators Gary Miller and Mark Winters at 9:20 p.m. Mendoza stated that he had arrived in town on Wednesday, May 8, with Brandy, his girlfriend and mother of their child. Brandy returned to Arizona on Friday while he remained in town at his mother's house at 1872 Grier Street. On the evening of May 10, he purchased some beer, went home, and he did not leave again until the following morning. While at home, he was visited by several friends, including Joseph Cesena. According to Ronald, the only persons in the house when he went to sleep were his brother Angel and a friend named Jaime.

Ronald Mendoza denied owning a pager. When confronted with the fact that a pager purchased by him had been recovered near the murder scene, he said that he bought a pager for a friend named Hector and that Hector paid the monthly pager bill. He did not know Hector very well and last saw him about a week and a half earlier. Ronald Mendoza also stated that he had no knowledge of the .45 caliber Remington bullets found on the trash can at his residence.

Angel Mendoza a.k.a. "Bandit," nineteen-year-old, Hispanic male

Angel Mendoza was also interviewed on the evening of May 11, at the Walnut Sheriff's Station by Investigators Miller and Winters. He said that on the evening of May 10, he went to bed between 9:30 and 10:00 p.m. and that his brother Ronald was not home at the time. He also said that he had a pager with an access number of 448-4098 and that Ronald got rid of his pager in January 1996. However, later in the interview he said Ronald had a pager with an access number of 448-4099 and that he and Ronald are responsible for their own pager bills. Angel also said that as recently as last week, he paged Ronald in Arizona on Ronald's pager.

> NOTE: Although Angel's statement conflicted with Ronald's statement in several respects, there was insufficient evidence at that time to arrest Ronald or Angel Mendoza. Both brothers left the Walnut Sheriff's station after they were interviewed. Ronald Mendoza returned to Lake Havasu, Arizona, on Monday, May 13, 1996.

THE HAPPY TOWN GANG

Joseph Cesena, Ronald Mendoza, and Angel Mendoza were all members of the Happy Town gang in Pomona, California. Gang investigators in Pomona were aware that the Happy Town gang made it extremely dangerous for someone to cooperate with law enforcement in the investigation of crimes committed by Happy Town gang members.

For example, a Happy Town gang member named Enrique Hernandez had been on trial for murder in Pomona Superior Court. During the investigation, another Happy Town gang member named Mario Torres told investigators that he was a witness to the murder which was committed by Enrique Hernandez. This statement was tape recorded by Pomona investigators. During the trial of Enrique Hernandez, Mario Torres refused to testify. However, his taped statement was played to the jury, and Hernandez was convicted of murder. Approximately one week later, the body of Mario Torres was found in Kellogg Park in Pomona. He had received numerous stab wounds in his upper chest and neck area, and his throat was slit from ear to ear.

The word on the street was that Torres was murdered because of the statement he had given to police in the Enrique Hernandez investigation. Gang members and others who lived in the area were aware of the Torres murder and were extremely reluctant to cooperate with law enforcement because of this murder.

OFFICER DANIEL TIMOTHY FRAEMBS

The funeral of Officer Daniel Timothy Fraembs took place on May 17, 1996. Hundreds of law enforcement officers from different agencies throughout the state of California attended the funeral.

Officer Fraembs was not certain of his actual date of birth. He believed his date of birth was October 30, 1958. He was born in Hong Kong. Shortly after his birth, with his umbilical cord still attached, he was abandoned at a beach in Hong Kong. His cries were overheard by a Hong Kong police officer who rescued him and took him to a hospital. He was thereafter placed in an orphanage.

At nine months of age, he was adopted by Donald and Dorothy Fraembs of Cincinnati, Ohio, and brought to the United States. Six months later, the Fraembses adopted a second child from Hong Kong, Danah Fraembs, who was about one year younger than her brother.

Donald Fraembs died of a heart attack when Daniel was fourteen years of age. Dorothy Fraembs did not remarry and raised the children on her own.

Daniel Fraembs became a citizen of the United States in August 1963, a few months before his fifth birthday. He grew up in Cincinnati and graduated from Forest Park High School in Cincinnati in 1977. Later that year, he enrolled at the University of Cincinnati. He completed his education in Southern California at Fullerton Community College.

In 1981, Fraembs joined the United States Marine Corps. He served in Beirut, where he saw action. He reached the rank of sergeant before his honorable discharge in 1985.

In September 1988, he joined the Orange County Sheriff's Department where he worked as a jailer. He was a member of the Sheriff's Department martial-arts team, which performed at charity events. On August 31, 1993, he became a member of the Pomona Police Department because he wanted an opportunity to "work the streets."

Officer Fraembs was not married. He was survived by his mother Dorothy and sister Danah, both of Cincinnati, Ohio. They were flown to Los Angeles to attend his funeral.

BREAKTHROUGH! JOHANNA FLORES

After she observed Ronald Mendoza shoot Officer Daniel Fraembs, Johanna Flores ran to her residence. She was unable to sleep. In the morning, she told her sister what had happened. Later in the morning, Johanna spoke to Ronald Mendoza over the telephone. He stated that he was a killer and did not care about what he had done because "it was just another day in the hood."

Later that day or the following day, Johanna told her parents what happened. Her father spoke with their family priest, Father Charles Gard, who offered to talk with Johanna. On May 15, Johanna spoke to Father Gard and told him about the shooting of Officer Fraembs and the involvement of Ronald Mendoza. Father Gard noticed that Johanna was "very upset" and "very distraught" yet she was very confident in what she was saying. Father Gard persuaded Johanna to talk to the police.

Father Gard contacted the District Attorney's Office and stated that the daughter of a member of his church had information about the killing of the officer but was afraid for her safety. Sheriff's Homicide investigators were apprised, and they interviewed Johanna on May 16, along with Deputy District Attorney Mark Arnold.

Although Johanna was concerned about her safety and that of her family, she agreed to be a witness. She believed that what Ronald Mendoza did was wrong and that he had the chance to run away but did not do so. At her request, the Pomona Police Department relocated her and her family.

Johanna Flores became the key witness in the prosecution's case against Ronald Mendoza.

WIRETAP ORDER

On May 15, 1996, Sheriff's Homicide investigators obtained a court order pursuant to the California wiretap statute to monitor and record telephone conversations over several telephones, including two telephones that were issued to 1872 Grier Street, Pomona, the residence of Ronald Mendoza's mother and step-father. Between May 15 and May 20, 1996, Mendoza made several calls to the telephones at this residence.

Ronald Mendoza was arrested on May 21, 1996, in Arizona, and he remained in custody in Arizona pending his extradition to California to face trial for the murder of Officer Fraembs. While in custody in Arizona, he made additional calls to his mother's residence. By then he realized that Johanna Flores would be a prosecution witness; the calls to his mother reflected that concern. On May 22, he told his mother to get rid of his orange and black jacket (Flores had told investigators that Mendoza was wearing a black jacket with an orange lining when he killed the officer). On May 24, Mendoza told his mother he wanted "Goon" (Flores) to be told that she "better realize what she's doing." Although complaining that Goon was "supposed to be gang, now she's fucking crumbling down." Mendoza told his mother "we gotta do something because if she's a witness, I'm gonna be gone." Mendoza also stated that "as far as she's willing to go, the police ain't going to protect her."

FELONY COMPLAINT AND PRELIMINARY HEARING

Deputy District Attorney Mark Arnold of CAPOS rolled out to the crime scene on the early morning of May 11, 1996, to provide legal assistance to investigators in the shooting death of Officer Daniel Fraembs. Arnold had the ideal background for a prosecutor in CAPOS. He had joined the Los Angeles County Sheriff's Department in 1972 and spent the next thirteen years as a deputy sheriff. He went to law school at night, passed the state bar examination, and joined the District Attorney's Office in 1985 as an entry-level prosecutor. He proved to be an excellent trial lawyer and successfully prosecuted serious gang cases as a member of the Hardcore Gang Division. In 1990, he became a member of CAPOS. In June 1995, Arnold obtained a death penalty verdict against the person who murdered Compton Police Officers Kevin Burrell and James MacDonald, as set forth in Chapter 3.

On May 21, 1996, Deputy District Attorney Mark Arnold filed a felony complaint charging Ronald Bruce Mendoza with one count of first-degree murder of Pomona Police Officer Daniel Timothy Fraembs. The complaint contained special circumstances allegations of murder of a police officer engaged in the performance of his duties and murder to prevent a lawful arrest. If either of these special circumstances allegations were proven, it made the defendant eligible for the death penalty.

Mendoza was arrested in Arizona on May 21, 1996. He was extradited back to Los Angeles on June 25th and arraigned on the murder charges in the Pomona Municipal Court on June 27th. A preliminary hearing was conducted in the case on August 19 and 20, 1996, before Judge S. Clark Moore in the Municipal Court of the Pomona Judicial District. Deputy District Attorney Mark Arnold was the prosecutor, and attorney Rayford Fountain represented the defendant. Johanna Flores was the key prosecution witness. Defendant Ronald Mendoza was bound over for the murder with all special allegations.

POST-PRELIMINARY HEARING

In a murder case in which special circumstances are alleged and proven, the penalty is either death or life in prison without the possibility of parole. The decision of whether death is the appropriate penalty is determined after the preliminary hearing by the District Attorney's Special Circumstances Evaluation Committee. Deputy District Attorney Mark Arnold prepared an eight-page memorandum to the committee in which he recommended that the death penalty was the appropriate punishment for Ronald Bruce Mendoza. The committee and the chairperson agreed, and the prosecution announced it would be seeking the death penalty in the case.

The trial was assigned to Judge Alfonso M. Bazan in the Pomona Superior Court. Deputy District Attorney Mark Arnold remained the prosecutor on the case. Attorney Rayford Fountain represented the defendant.

What follows is an overview of the principals and the charges at the trial.

PEOPLE v. RONALD BRUCE MENDOZA
Case KA032117

JUDGE:	The Honorable Alfonso M. Bazan
PROSECUTOR:	Mark Arnold, Deputy District Attorney Crimes Against Peace Officer Section (CAPOS)
DEFENSE ATTORNEY:	Rayford Fountain, Attorney at Law
CHARGES:	Murder in the First-Degree with Three Special Circumstances Allegations:

- Murder of Peace Officer Intentionally Killed in Performance of His Duties
- Murder to Prevent Lawful Arrest
- Murder Committed While Lying in Wait

LOCATION: Los Angeles Superior Court
                                   Pomona, East-Department F

NOTE: *The special circumstance allegation of murder committed while lying in wait was added after the preliminary hearing*

JURY TRIAL – TESTIMONY OF JOHANNA FLORES

Jury selection in the trial of Ronald Bruce Mendoza began on July 16, 1997. The jury was "death qualified" in that the jurors stated that they could return a verdict of death in an appropriate case. The jury was em-paneled on July 23, 1997.

The centerpiece of the prosecution case during the 1997 trial was the testimony of Johanna Flores. She testified in detail to the circumstances of the murder of Officer Daniel Fraembs and the role played by Ronald Mendoza, as follows:

She was nineteen-years-old at the time of the trial. She was divorced and had a two-year-old daughter from the marriage. She met Ronald Mendoza in February or March 1996 when she went with a girlfriend to Mendoza's residence on Grier Street. During this first meeting, Mendoza gave her his pager number and asked her to call him the following day. During the next three weeks, Flores paged Mendoza fifty or sixty times; he always called her in response to a page. They began a romantic relationship. Mendoza was known as "Box-er," and he referred to Flores as "Johanna" or "Goon."

By May 11, 1996, Flores and Mendoza had been together on about forty or fifty occasions. At almost every occasion she saw Mendoza with his beeper.

On the evening of May 10, 1996, Flores worked at Taco Bell from 4:00 p.m. until 11:00 p.m. Mendoza called Flores near the end of her shift and asked her to meet him and bring him some food to Tank's house. She met Mendoza at Tank's house where they had sex. Then they had an argument when Mendoza received a voicemail message from Brandy Valore, a woman with whom Mendoza had a child. During the argument, Flores hit Mendoza in the waist area and felt a gun there.

After the argument Mendoza made telephone contact with his friend Joseph Cesena, a member of the Happy Town gang with the moniker of "Sparky." Mendoza told Cesena that he and Flores would meet him by some railroad tracks and return to Tank's residence. Flores heard Mendoza tell Cesena that he should hurry to the meeting place since he had a gun and didn't want to get busted.

Johanna Flores and Ronald Mendoza then left Tank's residence to meet Cesena. On the way, they encountered Cherie Hernandez and Elva Arambula. Mendoza asked for, and received, a cigarette from one of the females. The two groups then moved on, away from each other. Flores and Mendoza met Cesena at the railroad tracks where he emerged from some bushes. They began walking to Tank's house.

As they walked, a bright light came on from behind them, illuminating the ground in front of them. It was a police patrol car, driving slowly down the street. Mendoza said, "Oh shit, the jura" ("Jura" meant "the cops"). The police car came to a stop behind the three pedestrians. The officer driving the car, who was the car's sole occupant, got out of the patrol car, leaving the spotlight turned on and the driver's door open. Mendoza in a low voice said, "Oh, shit. I got the gun." Flores and Cesena told Mendoza to run, but he remained where he was.

The officer asked, "How are you guys doing tonight?" Flores thought that the officer was "real nice" and that he had stopped them for a curfew check and nothing major. Mendoza demanded to know why they were being stopped. The officer told Flores and Mendoza to stand by the curb; and he directed Cesena, who was closest to him, to come over to the patrol car.

The officer began a pat-down search of Cesena.

In the meantime, Mendoza was standing directly behind Flores with his chest against her back and leaning forward, and she was forced to step off the curb with Mendoza still directly behind her. Flores felt Mendoza's hand sliding down between himself and the small of her back. Mendoza continued to move toward the officer, who was still patting down Cesena. When they got within six or seven feet of the officer, Mendoza pushed her aside and stretched out his arms holding the gun with both hands. Mendoza took another step or two toward the officer and pointed the gun toward the officer's upper body. From a distance of two or three feet, Mendoza fired once, striking the officer in the face. The officer put his arm out toward Flores, then fell to the ground, landing on his side near the open driver's door of the patrol car, and rolled over onto his back.

After shooting the officer, Mendoza pointed the gun at her upper torso and said, "Are you going to say anything?" Flores responded, "No, I didn't see nothing. I didn't hear nothing. I don't know nothing." Mendoza said, "I am going to ask you again," and again asked if she was going to say anything. Flores again replied that she "didn't see anything, hear anything, or know anything." Mendoza then said "Run."

Mendoza ran down the street, toward Mission Boulevard. Flores ran in the same direction, behind Mendoza. She lost sight of him shortly thereafter. Mendoza did not look back at Flores and did not wait for her to catch up with him. Cese-

na had already run away, back toward the bushes from which he had earlier emerged.

Flores reached her home where her daughter, her sister, and her sister's boyfriend were. She went to bed but could not sleep. She did not call 911 or the police to report the shooting, because she was afraid that Mendoza or his gang would do something to her.

JURY TRIAL - ADDITIONAL

In addition to the testimony of Johanna Flores, there was ample testimony and evidence that corroborated her testimony and independently established the guilt of the defendant, including the following:

- Jason Meyers and Dean Coleman established that about two weeks before the murder of Officer Fraembs, Meyers drove Mendoza to Coleman's residence where Mendoza purchased a Haskell .45 caliber handgun from Coleman for $150 or $155. Meyers and Mendoza then drove to a Big 5 Sporting Goods Store, where Mey-ers used Mendoza's money to purchase a green and yellow box of Remington .45 caliber bullets, which he gave to Mendoza.

- Cherie Hernandez and Elva Arambula testified to encountering Johanna Flores and Ronald Mendoza on the early morning of May 11, 1996. Hernandez gave Mendoza a cigarette and lit it for him. The two groups separated, and Mendoza and Flores continued toward the railroad tracks.

- Mendoza's pager was found near the body of Officer Fraembs.

- A spent shell casing was on the ground about twelve feet from the body, and an expended bullet lay in the grass about forty to fifty feet away. A senior criminalist with the Sheriff's Department testified that the casing was made by Remington Peters and designed for a .45-caliber semi-automatic weapon and was consistent with the expended bullet. The criminalist also testified that the projectile could have been fired from a Haskell .45-caliber semi-automatic weapon.

- A green and yellow Remington .45-caliber ammunition box bearing a Big 5 Sporting Goods price tag was found in the bedroom occupied by Mendoza's mother and stepfather. The box contained one .32 caliber bullet and an otherwise empty plastic ammunition tray, on which Mendoza's left thumbprint was found.

- A black nylon camera lens case containing seventeen Remington .45-caliber bullets was recovered from a trash can in the enclosed backyard of the residence occupied by Mendoza's mother and stepfather. The stepfather identified the lens case, but not the bullets. He had not seen the case for a year and did not know how it got into the trash can.

- After the murder, Mendoza sold the murder weapon to Joseph Silva for $100, telling him, "Hey, did you know I killed a cop?" Mendoza later decided to get the gun back, and his brother Angel retrieved the gun from Silva.

- Mendoza made some incriminating statements to his mother that were intercepted and recorded pursuant to a wiretap order.

CORONER'S TESTIMONY

On May 12, 1996, an autopsy was performed on the body of Officer Fraembs by Dr. James Ribe, a forensic pathologist and senior medical examiner with the Los Angeles County Coroner's Office. The officer was five feet, six inches tall. The cause of death was a single through-and-through gunshot wound to the head. The entry wound was located on the left side of the bony part of the bridge of the nose. The exit wound was located on the back of the head toward the right side and fairly low.

Dr. Ribe gave the opinion that the last sensations Officer Fraembs would have experienced in life were his observation of the gun pointed at him, the sight of the muzzle flash, and the sound of the explosion of the bullet being fired into his face. Dr. Ribe opined that Officer Fraembs did not feel any pain as a result of the gunshot wound to his head, and he "could have been dead within a very few seconds, two to three, maybe five seconds would be the most" Officer Fraembs' life could not have been saved after receiving the gunshot wound in the manner it was inflicted.

DEFENSE CASE

The defense called only one witness, a security guard who was on duty at Hughes Aircraft on Humane Way in Pomona on May 11, 1996. The witness testified that between 1:00 and 1:30 a.m. he observed a police car pass by his location on Humane Way at a slow speed and then drove out of his sight. Shortly thereafter he heard a gunshot and then a female voice screaming, "Let's get out of here" or "Let's move from here." He also thought he saw two males wearing dark clothing run toward an incinerator behind the building.

Ronald Mendoza did not testify.

CLOSING ARGUMENTS

The defense strategy was to attack the credibility of Johanna Flores, the prosecution's key witness. She was cross-examined regarding her gang affiliations, her drug and alcohol use, her sex life and her jealousy toward Mendoza's relationship with Brandy Valore, and her fights with Mendoza.

During closing arguments, defense attorney Rayford Fountain argued to the jury that Flores was a jealous, foul-mouthed, drug abusing, "hard-core home girl gang banger" who was wrongfully accusing Mendoza of murder because of his relationship with Valore.

Fountain also argued to the jury that even if they believed Mendoza was the shooter, he did not act with premeditation and should only be convicted of second-degree murder.

Fountain also contended that the special circumstance allegations of murder of a police officer in the performance of his duties and murder to avoid a lawful arrest did not apply because Officer Fraembs made an improper detention of Mendoza, Flores, and Cesena and therefore was not acting lawfully in performing his duties when he was killed. Prosecutor Mark Arnold effectively countered this contention in his closing argument, as follows:

> *"It is 1:30 in the morning and [Fraembs] elected to find out what is going on with these three people. Are these three motorists that have been stranded and are looking for help? Is this female who is in the presence of the two males, is she involuntarily in their company? Are these three people who are lost? Are these three people suspects who are looking for a vehicle to burglarize or perhaps a business to burglarize because, remember, this is an industrial street. Officer Fraembs doesn't know."*

JURY VERDICT

On August 13, 1997, the jury convicted defendant Ronald Bruce Mendoza of first-degree murder and found true the allegation that he personally used a firearm in commission of the murder. The jury also found true the three special circumstance allegations: the defendant intentionally killed a police officer in performance of his duties; he committed murder for the purpose of avoiding a lawful arrest; and he intentionally killed the victim by means of lying in wait.

Since the jury convicted Mendoza of first-degree murder with special circumstance allegations found true, a penalty phase was conducted in which the jury would decide whether the defendant should receive the death penalty or be sentenced to life imprisonment without the possibility of parole.

PENALTY PHASE

The penalty phase commenced on August 18, 1997. The prosecution presented evidence of a prior violent act committed by Ronald Mendoza as well as victim impact evidence.

The Prior Violent Act

On June 30, 1994, the victim drove to a friend's house in Pomona in his new 1994 blue Ford Thunderbird. While inside the house he heard more than ten gunshots fired from outside the house. He went on the porch to investigate and observed that his car had been shot up with numerous bullet holes to the vehicle. He observed three or four persons, including Ronald Mendoza, standing near his vehicle. Mendoza was holding an M-1 military rifle at his side. Fearing for his life, the victim ran back into the house. Mendoza and two of his fellow gang members followed the victim into the house. They beat him up and robbed him of some jewelry that he was wearing. After the beating, Mendoza told the victim words to the effect of, "Get the fuck out of the house before I kill you." The victim, fearing for his life, fled the house. Because of fear, the victim refused to prosecute.

Victim Impact Evidence

Dorothy Fraembs testified about her son, Officer Daniel Fraembs. She and her husband Donald adopted their son when he was nine months old. She was thrilled with the adoption and proud of her son as he grew up into a wonderful young man. She learned of her son's death the day before Mother's Day, when a police officer and a priest arrived at her residence. She stated that "I knew immediately why they were there" and "There was something that I had always hoped I would never see." Since her son's death, "there is a great big hole in my life and in my daughter's life."

When asked what she would tell her son if she could speak to him one more time, Mrs. Fraembs responded:

> "I'd say, he made us very proud to be part of his life and privileged to be his mother, and I always would say I hope you realize how much everybody—how much so many people loved him and how many people admired him. He was a very humble man. This is one of the things that so many people had said, he had so much humility, he could do so many things, but he was so humble. And I am not sure he knew how much everybody admired him. How much everybody loved him."

Darah Fraembs, Officer Fraembs's adopted sister, testified that when she learned of her brother's death, it felt like her whole world had been shattered. The pain of her brother's death had never left, and she thought about her brother every day.

Pomona Police Officers Mike Ezell and Douglas Wagaman had both worked with Officer Fraembs. They trained in martial arts together in Officer Fraembs's garage. They described Officer Fraembs as a shy man who loved his job and was a dedicated police officer. Officer Wagaman was especially impacted by the death of Officer Fraembs since he was on duty at the time and was one of the first officers to respond to the scene.

The defense presented Maria Christine Delgado, Ronald Mendoza's aunt, and Brandy Valore, the mother of Mendoza's child, as witnesses in mitigation.

Maria Delgado testified that Ronald Mendoza was born in December 1973, the second of three children born to her sister Lola Delgado. Ronald's father was Ronald Mendoza, Sr., and he also was the father of Ronald's younger brother Angel. Mr. Mendoza helped Lola raise Ronald and Angel; but after he returned from Vietnam, he developed a disease which left him paralyzed. After leaving Mr. Mendoza, Lola became addicted to heroin and served time in prison. Ronald and his brother and sister were raised by his grandparents in Pomona. Thereafter, Lola lived with Harry Lukens for a number of years; he did what he could for Lola's children. Mrs. Delgado asked the jury to spare her nephew's life.

Brandy Valore testified that she met Ronald Mendoza on July 15, 1994. They commenced a serious relationship. She was aware that he was on parole from the California Youth Authority. Approximately eighteen months later, she became pregnant. She stated that she and Mendoza planned on relocating to Lake Havasu, Arizona, where her mother resided, and raise a family, but Mendoza's parole agent refused permission for him to leave the state. Mendoza was present on April 27, 1996, when their daughter Raquel was born in a Phoenix hospital. She stated that Mendoza loved their daughter. She asked the jury to spare Mendoza's life so that their daughter would not lose her father. She admitted on cross-examination that she did not become aware of Mendoza's ongoing sexual relationship with another woman until after he was incarcerated.

The jurors were instructed and began deliberations on August 21, 1997. On August 22, 1997, the jury returned a verdict of death.

SENTENCING

On October 24, 1997, Judge Alfonso Bazan heard and denied the defendant's motion for a new trial, his motion to modify the conviction by re-

ducing it from first-degree murder to second-degree murder or by striking all of the special circumstances, his motion to reduce the sentence to
life without the possibility of parole, and his motion to continue the sentencing hearing. The court did strike the lying in wait special circumstance. Judge Bazan then imposed the death sentence.

SUPREME COURT DECISION

Every defendant who receives a sentence of death has an automatic appeal
to the California Supreme Court. On November 10, 2011, the California
Supreme Court issued its decision in *People v. Ronald Bruce Mendoza*, 52
Cal 4th 1056 (2011).

In the opinion written by Justice Baxter, the court unanimously affirmed the first-degree murder conviction and the death sentence. The
Court found the detention and pat-down of Mendoza and his two com-
panions was lawful. The Court reinstated the lying in wait special circumstance allegation.

In finding sufficient evidence of deliberate and premeditated first-
degree murder, the opinion stated the following:

> *The record contains substantial evidence that the killing did
> not result from an unconsidered or rash impulse. Although
> defendant did not initiate the contact with Officer Fraembs,
> Flores' testimony amply supported the inference that defend-
> ant devised a plan to kill Fraembs once the officer indicated
> he would conduct a weapons search. As Fraembs began his
> pat down of Sparky, defendant acted as if he were complying
> with Fraembs's direction to sit down on the curb. By using
> Flores as a shield and carefully controlling her movements,
> defendant was able to approach Fraembs without attracting
> attention and to maneuver himself to a position of advantage
> over the unsuspecting officer. Once defendant got within six*

or seven feet of the officer, he was able to draw his gun while still screened by Flores. Defendant then pushed her aside and quickly stepped even closer to Fraembs. He took aim with both arms extended and shot the officer in the face. Defendant's plan proved successful, as Fraembs was taken utterly by surprise and had no opportunity to reach for his own weapons. People v. Mendoza 52 Cal 4ᵗʰ 1056 at page 1070.

LESSONS LEARNED

Trainers, supervisors and police leaders must never lose sight of the need to reinforce that officers should announce by radio their location and the nature of their activity when they initiate a field stop. This is especially true for single-officer units (but we should not forget that both partners in a two-officer unit sometimes get murdered, too).

In this tragic case, Officer Fraembs was working alone. He was patrolling an industrial area in the middle of the night, where there was little traffic or activity. He saw two men and a woman walking and elected to stop and investigate. He did not radio his location or the nature of the stop. He did not request a back-up unit. Yet, he initiated a frisk search of one of the subjects (Cesena). For reasons we cannot know, Officer Fraembs was either unaware of, or he allowed killer Mendoza and girlfriend Flores to approach to within a few feet, where he was searching Cesena. Mendoza then quickly closed in and killed Officer Fraembs with one shot to the head.

It is unclear how much time elapsed between the time that Officer Fraembs last communicated with the dispatcher and the call at 1:37 a.m. from the private citizen that an officer was down. This raises the concern of whether the radio dispatcher was aware that Officer Fraembs had not been heard from in a long time; and whether the agency had a system requiring dispatchers to check with field units at least once per hour.

The nature of the job is that field officers must be given broad discretion about initiating field investigations. There are so many things that can get an officer's attention in the field that cannot be placed into a single box and tied up with a bow. However, at minimum, an agency should require (and supervisors should enforce) a rule that requires the officer to announce their location and nature of the activity when they make a stop.

Another recurring problem in the culture of many agencies is that officers do not request back-up as often as they should. Trainers and supervisors must often talk about incidents where doing so made a positive difference in the outcome, as well as talk about the incidents that ended in tragedy--like this one.

The Fraembs case, and too many other similar tragedies, prove the point about the importance of broadcasting the location and reason for the stop, and a back-up request when warranted. In addition, it is important to realize that when officers make a location and activity broadcast, the dispatcher and the other officers can hear whether there is anything unusual or urgent about the sound of the officer's voice that indicates a problem that would cause back-up to respond, whether or not the officer requested it.

Finally, it must be noted that a thorough search outward from the immediate crime scene yielded helpful results in this case. A K-9 unit found Cesena hiding nearby several hours after the killing. There was also the recovery near the crime scene of the pager that had been purchased by a person giving Mendoza's name and home address.

COMMENTARY OF STEVE COOLEY

One common thread in the chapters in this book is the outstanding work performed by the law enforcement agencies involved in the investigation of the murders of police officers. Many of these cases could not be solved and successfully prosecuted without the efforts of these investigating officers.

However, it often takes more than excellent investigation for a case to be provable in a court of law. Civilian witnesses must be located and interviewed to determine if their testimony can result in a successful prosecution. There is nothing more frustrating for a detective than a case in which the identity of a perpetrator has been established, but the case cannot be proven in court because of a lack of witnesses.

The murder of Officer Daniel Fraembs could not have been solved or successfully prosecuted without civilian witness Johanna Flores. The detectives had reached a virtual dead end in their investigation until Flores came forward to identify Ronald Mendoza as the perpetrator. Later she was the key witness against him.

There are many cases in which civilian witnesses, at great peril to themselves and their families, cooperate with law enforcement in solving an important case. However, I know of no case in which a witness played a greater role in bringing a dangerous criminal to justice than in the murder of Officer Daniel Fraembs and the unselfish and courageous performance of Johanna Flores.

Officer Daniel T. Fraembs

Officer Daniel T. Fraembs who was known as one of Pomona's most well informed officers on Asian gangs was shot and killed in the early hours of Saturday, May 11, 1996, while checking three subjects in an industrial area within the City of Pomona. Officer Daniel T. Fraembs was the first Police Officer in the 108 year history of the Pomona Police Department to be gunned down in the line of duty. Following an extensive search for the suspects, the primary suspect was identified to be a 22 year old Pomona gang member who was located in Kingman, Arizona and was arrested on May 22, 1996. The suspect was later convicted and received the death sentence.

Daniel was born in Hong Kong. A Hong Kong Police Officer was on foot patrol in the beach area and heard the sounds of a crying baby. Daniel was found abandoned on the beach and the Police Officer turned Daniel over to a local orphanage. At nine months of age Daniel was adopted by Donald and Dorothy Fraembs of Cincinnati, Ohio. In August of 1963 Daniel Timothy Fraembs, became a citizen of the United States of America. Daniel graduated from Forest Hills High School in Cincinnati, Ohio in 1977. In the fall of that year Daniel enrolled at the University of Cincinnati and later completed his education at Fullerton Community College.

In 1981, Daniel T. Fraembs joined the United States Marine Corps, where he excelled and was a highly decorated Marine receiving numerous medals, badges, citations and campaign ribbons while in the service. Daniel had obtained the rank of Sergeant prior to receiving his honorable discharge in 1985.

In September 1988, Daniel T. Fraembs was appointed to the Orange County Sheriffs Department, where Daniel worked for five years before joining the Pomona Police Department. Daniel T. Fraembs is survived by his mother, Dorothy Fraembs and sister, Darah Fraembs of Cincinnati, Ohio.

DATE OF BIRTH: OCTOBER 30, 1958
APPOINTED: AUGUST 31, 1993
END OF WATCH: MAY 11, 1996

Officer Fraembs and his police vehicle

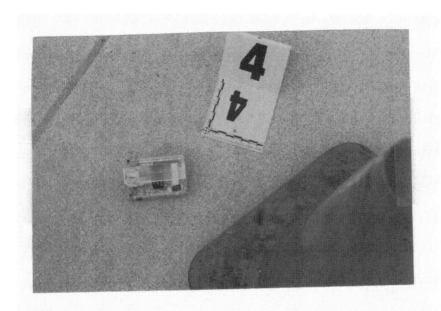

Ronald Mendoza's pager was found near the crime scene

Aerial views of industrial area where Officer Fraembs was shot

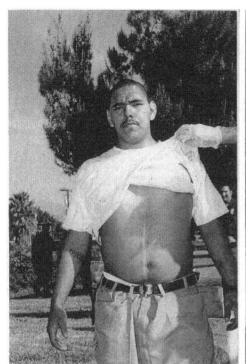

Joseph Cesena was arrested near the murder scene hiding in the bushes near an abandoned city incinerator

Ronald Mendoza was arrested in Arizona and extradited back to Los Angeles

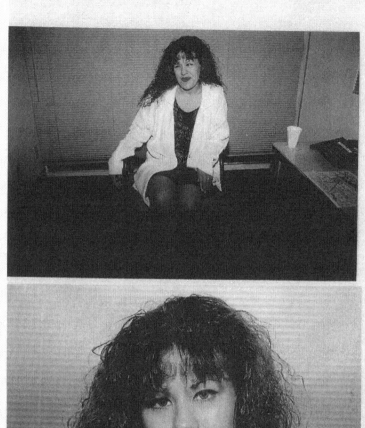

Johanna Flores was the key prosecution witness

CHAPTER SIX

Officer Filbert Cuesta, Jr.

Los Angeles Police Department

"The Price of Perfect Justice"

August 9, 1998

OFFICER FILBERT HENRY CUESTA, JR.

FILBERT HENRY CUESTA, JR., was born in La Mirada, California, on November 8, 1971. He was the son of Filbert Henry Cuesta, Sr., and Rosalia Cuesta. He grew up in Whittier, California, and received his primary education at St. Paul of the Cross. He attended St. Paul's High School in Santa Fe Springs, graduating in 1989, and he received an AA degree from Cerritos College in 1992. At the time of his death, he was attending California State University in Long Beach studying to get a bachelor's degree.

Officer Cuesta joined the Los Angeles Police Department on March 21, 1994. He was assigned to the department's anti-gang Community Resources Against Street Hoodlums (CRASH) operating from the Southwest Division.

He lived in Norwalk with his wife, Sylvia, and daughters, Samantha, eighteen-months-old, and four-week-old Sierra. He had taken paternity leave after the birth of his second daughter. He had been back at work for only three days when he was shot and killed in an ambush murder.

CATARINO GONZALEZ, JR.

Catarino Gonzalez was born in Los Angeles on March 17, 1978. He was the son of Catarino Gonzales, Sr., and Teresa Gonzalez. He attended Cheviot Hills High School and lived with his parents at 5462 Smiley Drive, Los Angeles.

Catarino Gonzalez was an "18th Street" gang member affiliated with the "Smiley Drive Gangsters" or "TMS" clique. His gang monikers were "Termite" and "Cat." Family members and associates sometimes saw him in possession of a Glock nine-millimeter pistol that he occasionally carried on his person.

On July 10, 1997, at about 6:00 p.m., he was standing on the southeast corner of Hauser Boulevard and Stanley Drive talking to a young female when shots were fired in their direction from a passing vehicle. Both

Gonzalez and the female sustained non-fatal gunshot wounds. Gonzalez received three gunshot wounds to his right shoulder area. He received medical treatment for his injuries; and, for a period of time, he had limited use of his right arm.

Gonzalez had been arrested for various narcotics violations. His most recent arrest was on April 1, 1998, for possession of cocaine with the intent to sell. Acting on a tip that Gonzalez was dealing cocaine, officers observed him in a group of six males. When Gonzalez observed the officers, he tossed a clear plastic bag over a wrought iron fence. Officers retrieved the baggie which contained thirteen rocks of cocaine. Gonzalez had forty-seven dollars in his left front pocket which was consistent with sales of cocaine. Officer Filbert Cuesta was one of the officers who participated in the arrest of Gonzalez.

As a result of this arrest, Catarino Gonzalez was charged with possession of cocaine for sale in case number BA166331. He entered a guilty plea to the charge and received a sentence of 120 days in county jail with three years formal probation and a suspended state prison sentence of three years. If Gonzalez were found in violation of probation during the probationary period, the three years suspended sentence could be imposed.

In early 1998, Officer Gary Copeland of Southwest Bureau CRASH was on patrol when he observed a group of four or five young male Hispanics, known to him to be 18th Street gang members. They were loitering on the street and drinking in public. Officer Copeland approached them, counseled them about drinking in public (a violation of the Los Angeles Municipal Code), and released them. As the group walked away, he observed a photograph on the ground. It was a photograph of Catarino Gonzalez holding what appeared to be a Glock semi-automatic handgun. He took custody of the photograph and later placed it in the 18th Street file cabinet at the Southwest Division CRASH office.

On August 3, 1998, at about 1:00 a.m., less than a week before the murder of Officer Cuesta, Officer Copeland arrested Catarino Gonzalez for drinking in public and for a possible arrest warrant. At the Southwest

Station, it was determined the arrest warrant was not for Gonzalez. He was cited for drinking in public and released. Gonzalez was upset since he had to get home on his own from Southwest Station in the early morning hours. The following evening Officer Copeland observed freshly painted graffiti with Gonzalez' moniker, "Termite," and the word "police" crossed out. [In local gang culture, crossed-out words in graffiti signified that the person or group so marked was to be killed.]

AUGUST 8-9, 1998

On August 8, 1998, Officers Filbert Cuesta and Richard Gabaldon were assigned to Southwest Division CRASH working the mid-p.m. shift starting at 6:00 p.m. They were in full LAPD uniform driving a marked black and white police vehicle. Officer Cuesta was twenty-six-years-of-age with four years in the department, and Officer Gabaldon was twenty-seven-years-old with three years on the job.

Community Resources Against Street Hoodlums (CRASH) was a specialized unit designed to gather gang intelligence and monitor gang activity in certain specific geographical areas. Officers Cuesta and Gabaldon were assigned to the west side of the Southwest Division monitoring street gangs that included the 18th Street gang. Their primary duties included gathering gang intelligence, identifying gang members, arresting gang members wanted on warrants, and assisting in the service of search warrants. Both officers had conducted several field interviews of Catarino Gonzalez, and Officer Cuesta had participated in the arrest of Gonzalez on April 1, 1998. They knew that he was a member of the 18th Street gang with the moniker of "Termite."

Officer Cuesta had been on paternity leave after the birth of his baby daughter; this this was his third night back on the job. Officer Cuesta told Officer Gabaldon that he was concerned about some graffiti on Hauser Boulevard and Homestead Street in which the word "police" had been written on the wall and a line had been drawn through it. The moniker on the wall was "Termite." The officers knew that when a gang member writes something with a line through it, it meant the gang intended to kill someone. Officer Cuesta mentioned that Catarino Gonzalez, a.k.a. "Termite," was on active probation and they should pick him up if they saw him.

Shortly after midnight, they drove westbound on Carlin Street, west of Cochran Street. They observed several gang members in the area of 5331 and 5333 Carlin Street and heard loud music and saw flashing lights at the location. Officer Cuesta was driving the police car, which he parked at the location. Both officers exited the vehicle and approached the gate at the location. They were met by someone who identified herself as Maria Guzman. She stated that she had just gotten married, and she was having a wedding reception in the patio area between the front residence (5331 Carlin Street) and the rear residence (5333 Carlin Street). The officers told her the music was too loud, there were gang members at the location, and she would have to close the party. Mrs. Guzman replied that she was tired, she wanted everyone to leave, there were a lot of people there who were not invited, including gang members, and that she would close the party down.

Maria Guzman stated that she would tell everyone to leave, but she doubted anyone would come out the front as long as the officers were there. The officers returned to their police car and decided to drive slowly around the block to give people a chance to leave the party. Officer Cuesta drove slowly away from the location, at approximately five to ten miles an hour. In the meantime, they called for additional CRASH units to help break up the party.

Officers Cuesta and Gabaldon completed circling the block and then parked the police vehicle in the intersection of Carlin Street and Duray Place, approximately three residences from the location of the party. The police car was in the middle of the street with the motor running while the officers waited for the other CRASH units to respond.

Officer Gabaldon was the passenger officer; he began to exit the vehicle to get their helmets. Suddenly, he heard gunshots being fired from a distance behind the rear of the vehicle. He heard a continuous popping noise in rapid succession; and he could see rounds sparking, hitting next to the police car and sailing by the passenger door. He estimated that twelve to fifteen shots were fired at him and his partner.

Officer Gabaldon slid down in his seat so he was not a visible target, and unholstered his gun. He heard Officer Cuesta say, "Aw fuck." He heard the back window being shot out, and the police car lunged forward. Officer Gabaldon believed Officer Cuesta was going to drive out of the danger zone, but instead, the police car crashed into a parked vehicle. Officer Gabaldon looked at Officer Cuesta and saw that his partner was slumped in the driver's seat with his head down and his chin on his chest. He was bleeding profusely from a wound to his forehead.

Officer Gabaldon stepped out of the car and looked in the direction of Carlin and Cochran Streets from where the shots had come. He saw three or four Hispanic males running off, but he did not get a good look at them. He fired five or six shots in their direction and moved to the inside of the police car to reach Officer Cuesta. He could see that Officer Cuesta had been shot through the rear of the head with an exit through the forehead. He put out an "officer needs help" call, giving the unit location and stating:

> "CRASH 45. Officer needs help. Shots fired. Officer down, and I need an ambulance to respond."

Officer Gabaldon then attended to his partner by putting pressure on the wound to stop the bleeding. Responding CRASH units arrived at the scene; and they assisted Officer Gabaldon in removing Officer Cuesta from the line of fire. An ambulance arrived, and Officer Cuesta was placed in the ambulance where he was treated by paramedics. Officer Gabaldon attempted to enter the ambulance, but was told to remain at the scene to give information to the command post. Later in the morning, he did a reenactment of the entire incident to the detectives assigned to the investigation.

Officer Cuesta was transported by ambulance to Cedars-Sinai Medical Center Hospital. He was admitted into the Intensive Care Unit and subsequently died at 4:16 a.m. on August 9, 1998.

CRIME SCENE INVESTIGATION

Responding units established a perimeter around the crime scene. A command post was established at Adams Boulevard and Redondo Boulevard. Personnel from eleven patrol divisions, three traffic divisions, Operations-Central Bureau CRASH, South Bureau Homicide, and Metropolitan Division responded to the incident. An extensive search located numerous witnesses and possible suspects within the perimeter. Approximately 100 people were transported to Southwest and 77th Divisions to be interviewed by detectives.

Detectives from LAPD's Robbery-Homicide Division conducted an investigation of the shooting location. The investigation disclosed Officers Cuesta and Gabaldon had parked their black and white police vehicle facing westbound in the intersection of Carlin Street and Duray Place, approximately three residences from the party. The rear window of the police vehicle had been shot out, and there were four bullet impacts observed on the vehicle.

The shooting location was the northwest corner of the intersection of Cochran Avenue and Carlin Street, on the sidewalk. The distance from the shooting location to the police vehicle was approximately 147 feet. Ten nine-millimeter "PMC" brand and one nine-millimeter "Winchester" brand cartridge cases were found at the shooting location, indicating that a total of eleven shots had been fired. A projectile was recovered in the headliner of the police car; it appeared to be nine-millimeter. According to firearms examiners, the cartridge casings at the shooting location were most likely fired from a Glock nine-millimeter pistol.

FOLLOW-UP INVESTIGATION

Detectives Richard Aldahl and Tom Mathew of the LAPD's Robbery-Homicide Division were assigned to lead the investigation into the death of Officer Filbert Cuesta. The Robbery-Homicide Division was considered the elite investigative division in the Los Angeles Police Department and contained many of its best investigators. Many of these detectives assisted in the investigation.

As previously indicated, in the two to three days following the murder of Officer Cuesta, detectives conducted approximately 100 interviews. Most of these interviews were of little or no value, but some provided the detectives with valuable information.

One important witness was seventeen-year-old Agapito Negron, who was interviewed by Detectives Richard Aldahl and John Garcia on August 9, 1998, at 11:45 a.m. Negron admitted he was a member of the 18th Street gang and that he had known "Termite" (Catarino Gonzalez) and "Casper" (Luis Antonio Cisneros) for years. On August 9, 1998, at approximately 12:30 a.m., he was at his rear "shack" at 2653 Cochran Avenue when he heard a series of shots fired near his residence. He went outside and observed "Termite" and "Casper" running "fast as hell" on Cochran Avenue. "Termite" was securing a black handgun in his waistband. Negron further stated that he observed "Termite" running between the houses next to his position, climb over the rear yard fence, and enter his (Termite's) sister's residence at 2642 Dunsmuir Avenue. He also saw "Casper" run to his residence at 2664 Cochran Avenue.

As a result of the information provided by Agapito Negron, detectives obtained a search warrant to search 2642 Dunsmuir Avenue, the residence of the sister of Catarino Gonzalez. This search was conducted on the afternoon of August 9, 1998, by Detective Buck Henry and his partner Detective Mike Berchem. Among the items of evidence recovered were a California identification card for Catarino Gonzalez, Jr., and 154 rounds of nine-millimeter ammunition in two plastic bags. The ammunition was found in the storage shed in the rear yard of the residence. A number of the rounds of ammunition were manufactured by PMC and Winchester;

the same manufacturers of the expended shell casings recovered at the shooting scene. Joel Loza, the brother-in-law of Catarino Gonzalez, told the detectives that he was not aware of this ammunition on his property.

Officer Copeland provided Detective Aldahl with the photograph depicting Catarino Gonzalez holding the black semi-automatic weapon, which appeared to be a Glock. Witnesses confirmed that Gonzalez had attended the wedding party, and at least one person saw a Glock handgun in his possession at the party. Other witnesses stated that they had observed Gonzalez in possession of a Glock handgun on prior occasions.

Detectives wanted to interview Catarino Gonzalez, but he could not be located. They contacted Joel Loza, who stated that he had not seen Gonzalez since the officer was killed. They asked for Loza's help in locating Gonzalez and to tell him that detectives wanted to interview him. On the evening on August 11, 1998, Loza contacted Detective Buck Henry and informed him that Catarino Gonzalez was willing to meet with detectives. Loza agreed to transport Gonzalez to the Robbery-Homicide Division. On August 11, 1998, at 9:50 p.m., Loza and Gonzalez arrived at Parker Center [LAPD Downtown Los Angeles headquarters] and were escorted to the Robbery-Homicide Division. At Loza's request, Gonzalez was photographed to show that he had no injuries before talking to police. Gonzalez was then taken to an interview room.

INTERVIEWS OF CATARINO GONZALEZ
First Interview

Catarino Gonzalez was first interviewed by Detectives Aldahl and Henry at the Robbery-Homicide Division at Parker Center on August 11, 1998, beginning at 10:35 p.m. The interview was electronically recorded. Gonzalez was advised of his rights, waived them, and agreed to talk to the detectives. He admitted that he was at the wedding reception. He stated that he heard gunshots while he was dancing and fled over the back gate. He ran to his sister's house and stayed there overnight. Gonzalez denied shooting

Officer Cuesta and denied having a gun at the reception. He knew there was a photograph of him holding a gun, but he did not know the name of the "homie" who sold the gun to him. The detectives asked him if he was willing to take a lie detector test. He replied:

> "...if for anything you guys are going to charge me, I want to talk to a public defender, too, for any little thing."

The detectives continued to talk to Gonzalez, and he agreed to submit to a polygraph examination on August 12, 1998. He was then arrested and booked for the murder of Officer Filbert Cuesta.

Second Interview (Polygraph Examination)

On August 12, 1998, at 12:30 p.m., Catarino Gonzalez submitted to a polygraph examination at the Scientific Investigation Division, Polygraph Section. The examination was conducted by polygraph examiner Ervin Youngblood, a civilian employee of the Los Angeles Police Department. The interview was electronically recorded. Prior to the examination, Gonzalez acknowledged that the investigators had advised him of his rights and that he had waived his rights. He agreed to talk to Youngblood.

Youngblood gave Gonzalez a detailed description of how the polygraph machine worked and encouraged him to be upfront and honest about what happened. On several occasions, he appealed to Gonzalez' sense of decency and encouraged him to "do the right thing."

In response to Youngblood's question regarding what was going through his mind at the time of the crime, Gonzalez responded, "I just wanted to scare him away." He subsequently stated that he acted alone, shot at the officers from the corner, and threw his gun away as he fled the scene. Youngblood asked him if he intended to shoot Officer Cuesta or was merely "shooting at the car." Gonzalez responded, "I was just shooting."

The interview terminated when Gonzalez asked to call his mother, and Youngblood left the room to get the detectives.

Third Interview

Detective Aldahl went into the interrogation room after Youngblood's departure and had a further conversation with Catarino Gonzalez. The conversation was also electronically recorded.

Detective Aldahl pressed Gonzalez about details of the crime. Gonzalez stated that he could not remember where he got the gun or how many rounds he fired at the police car. He admitted shooting at the police car and stated, "My intent wasn't to kill him. My intent wasn't to kill a cop." He stated that the shooting was the result of drunkenness, stupidity, and a desire to scare the officers.

After the police interrogation, Gonzalez met his mother, Theresa Gonzalez. They spoke in Spanish in the presence of Detective Garcia. He told his mother that he was not the shooter and that the police were lying when they stated that he was.

FILING OF CHARGES

On August 14, 1998, Deputy District Attorney Barbara Turner of CAPOS filed a criminal complaint charging Catarino Gonzalez, Jr., with two counts under case number BA172833. Count one alleged the first-degree murder of Los Angeles Police Officer Filbert Cuesta, Jr. Count two alleged the premeditated attempted murder of Los Angeles Police Officer Richard Gabaldon. There were firearm use enhancements to each count.

Regarding the murder of Officer Cuesta, the special circumstance was alleged that the victim was engaged in the performance of his duties as a peace officer at the time of the murder. If found true, this special circumstance made Catarino Gonzalez eligible for the death penalty.

FURTHER INVESTIGATION
Autopsy

On the morning of August 10, 1998, an autopsy was performed on the body of Filbert Cuesta. The autopsy took place at the Los Angeles County Coroner's Office and was performed by Doctor Eugene Carpenter, Deputy Medical Examiner. He ascribed the cause of death to "gunshot wound to the head, through and through." There were no bullet or bullet fragments recovered during the autopsy. The entrance wound was in the right rear side of the head, and the exit wound was the forehead between the eyebrows. The bullet passed through the brain, causing severe damage. In the opinion of Dr. Carpenter, it was a distant range gunshot wound.

Wedding Reception Photographs

Robert Lopez was a photographer hired by Maria and Fernando Guzman to photograph their wedding and reception. Lopez used seven rolls of film to photograph the events; he gave Detective R. King the undeveloped film. Detective King took the rolls of film to the LAPD's photo lab, where they were developed. He then provided Detective Richard Aldahl with a copy of the photographs. There were some photographs depicting Catarino Gonzalez at the wedding reception wearing a black shirt and gray khaki pants.

A second search warrant was served at 2642 Dunsmuir Avenue, the residence of Joel and Araceli Loza. At this location, Detective Henry recovered a black short sleeve "Dickies" shirt and a pair of gray "Ben Davis" pants on the upper shelf in the family room. Joel Loza told Detective Henry the clothing belonged to his wife's brother, Catarino Gonzalez. The clothing appeared to be the same type worn by Catarino Gonzalez at the wedding reception. The clothing was submitted to the crime lab for analysis, and gunshot residue particles were recovered from the clothing.

Wedding Reception Video

There was also a videotape of the wedding and subsequent reception. Detectives obtained the original of the videotape on August 20, 1998, and had copies made at the LAPD Electronics Section. The videotape depicted Catarino Gonzalez at the wedding reception. There appeared to be the outline of an object on his left side. Detectives believed the object might be a handgun. The video was taken to the National Law Enforcement and Corrections Technology Center in El Segundo to determine whether the videotape could be enhanced to verify a weapon under Gonzalez' shirt. However, the enhancements were inconclusive to prove the existence of a handgun.

PRELIMINARY HEARING

Deputy District Attorney Darren Levine of CAPOS was selected to prosecute the case against Catarino Gonzalez. He presented the prosecution case at the preliminary hearing that took place on June 8, 9 and 14, 1999, before Judge Elva Soper. Catarino Gonzalez was represented by defense attorney Michael Anton. Prosecutor Levine called only five witnesses at the preliminary hearing as follows:

1. *Officer Richard Gabaldon.* He was Filbert Cuesta's partner on August 8 and 9, 1998, and the victim in Count Two. He testified to the circumstances involving the shooting death of Officer Cuesta.

2. *Detective Ewing Kwock.* He was one of the detectives from the Robbery-Homicide Division who responded to the crime scene in the early morning hours of August 9, 1998. He described the shooting location, including the location and condition of the police car and the presence of eleven cartridge cases at the northwest corner of Cochran Avenue and Carlin Street.

3. *Officer Gary Copeland.* He was assigned to South Bureau CRASH with Officer Filbert Cuesta. He knew Catarino Gonzalez to be an 18th Street gang member. He testified to the April 1, 1998, arrest of Gonzalez; to the recovery of the photograph of Gonzalez holding the Glock handgun; to the August 3, 1998, arrest of Gonzalez for drinking in public; and to the graffiti on the wall with "police" crossed out.

4. *Sylvia.* Civilian witness Sylvia Thomas was allowed to testify, identifying herself as just "Sylvia," because of threats made against her. She had been relocated to another residence under a witness protection program because of concerns about her safety. She testified that on the early morning of August 9, 1998, she was living in an apartment building on Cochran Avenue near the intersection of Carlin Street. Shortly after midnight, she was standing on her balcony and saw a police car parked on Carlin Street with two officers inside. She noticed three men walking down Cochran Avenue toward Carlin Street. One of the men was the defendant, Catarino Gonzalez. When they reached the corner, Gonzalez stepped forward, raised his hands, and starting shooting. After the shooting stopped, the three men ran from the scene. "Sylvia" positively identified Catarino Gonzalez as the shooter.

5. *Agapito Negron.* Negron testified that he knew Catarino Gonzalez since they were both 18th Street gang members. He took the photograph of Gonzalez holding the Glock handgun and saw him carrying the Glock on a couple of occasions, including the wedding reception. Prosecutor Levine asked Negron the following:

> Q.   *Did you notice anyone on the corner*
>   *of Cochran and Carlin Street?*
> A.   *Yes*
> Q.   *Who was that?*
> A.   *I didn't get a good look at them. It was dark.*
>   *(Preliminary hearing transcript, page 248.)*

In his testimony, Negron refused to identify Gonzalez as the shooter, even though he had told detectives on numerous occasions that Gonzalez was the shooter. He admitted telling the detectives that Gonzalez was the shooter but claimed the police "made him say it."

Prosecutor Darren Levine made a tactical decision not to introduce any of Catarino Gonzalez' statements that he shot at the police car. There was enough evidence to bind the defendant over for trial without the introduction of the defendant's statements. Litigation into the admissibility of the statements could wait until the actual trial.

On June 14, 1998, Judge Elva Soper found the evidence sufficient for the case to go to trial. She ordered Catarino Gonzalez to appear in Department 100, the master calendar criminal court, for arraignment and plea.

PRE-TRIAL EVENTS

The Los Angeles County District Attorney's Office Special Circumstances Committee, chaired by a high-ranking member of the District Attorney's Office, carefully considers and evaluates the murder cases in which special circumstances are alleged. It decides in which of these cases the death penalty will be sought.

This evaluation process takes place after the preliminary hearing, so that the committee can be made aware of the nature of the evidence presented at a judicial proceeding. Defense attorneys may provide information and materials to the committee to assist in the committee's decision-making process.

After input from the Special Circumstances Committee, the chairman decided the prosecution would seek the death penalty against Catarino Gonzalez, Jr.

TRIAL OVERVIEW

The criminal trial of Catarino Gonzalez was assigned to Judge Robert J. Perry on the security floor of the Criminal Courts Building in downtown Los Angeles. Below is an overview of the trial.

PEOPLE v. CATARINO GONZALEZ
Case BA172833

JUDGE:	The Honorable Robert J. Perry
PROSECUTORS:	Darren Levine, Deputy District Attorney
	Loni Peterson, Deputy District Attorney
DEFENSE ATTORNEYS:	Michael Anton, Attorney at Law
	David Evans, Attorney at Law
CHARGES:	Count I – First-degree murder of Officer Filbert Cuesta
	• Special circumstances that the vic-tim was a peace officer engaged in the performance of his duties; that the murder was committed to avoid a lawful arrest; and that it was committed by means of lying in wait
	Count II -- Attempted first-degree mur-der of Officer Richard Gabaldon
MISCELLANEOUS:	If any one of the special circumstances were proven, the defendant would be eli-gible for the death penalty

MOTION TO SUPPRESS DEFENDANT'S STATEMENTS

The critical legal issue in the case against Catarino Gonzalez was the admissibility of the statements to detectives and to the polygraph operator. The attorneys for Gonzalez made a motion to suppress these statements on the grounds that they were obtained in violation of the *Miranda* decision and its progeny.

The *Miranda* decision was rendered by the United States Supreme Court and created a rule of constitutional magnitude. *Miranda* held that law enforcement officers must advise an accused of certain rights prior to questioning. Before an interrogation, the suspect must waive his or her rights and agree to speak to the officers. If a suspect asserts his or her rights to counsel during questioning, the interrogation must cease. However, the accused must clearly assert the right to counsel. Any statements made by a suspect after the assertion of his or her rights must be suppressed and cannot be used by the prosecution in its case-in-chief.

Before trial, Judge Robert Perry conducted a full-scale hearing into the defense motion to suppress the statements. The defense conceded that the defendant had initially been advised of his rights and had waived them. However, the defense argued that Gonzalez had invoked his right to counsel when he told the detectives, "If for anything you guys are going to charge me, I want to talk to a public defender, too, for any little thing."

The prosecution countered that Gonzalez' statement was ambiguous; although he made reference to a public defender, he never specifically asked for one.

At the hearing on the motion, four police officers testified that each had arrested the defendant on a prior occasion, and that on each occasion he had been advised of his *Miranda* rights. On two occasions, Gonzalez waived his rights and spoke to the officers. On the third occasion, he was given his rights but was not asked any further questions, although the record was unclear as to whether he had invoked his right to counsel. On the fourth occasion, Gonzalez asserted his right to counsel and was not questioned further.

Judge Perry denied the defendant's motion, concluding that his references regarding an attorney were ambiguous. He noted that Gonzalez was "an experienced person in terms of contact with the police."

Judge Perry stated the following in support of his ruling:

> *"This defendant well knew his Miranda rights even though he never had been suspected of killing a police officer. He had many contacts with the police. He knew what his rights were. There was ample opportunity during this interview for him to say, hey, that is it. I don't want to talk to you guys anymore. He never said that in a clear fashion as I believe required by the authorities."*

JURY TRIAL

Trial began in Judge Robert Perry's courtroom in April 2001 with jury selection. The jury was made aware that the prosecution was seeking the death penalty for the defendant, Catarino Gonzalez, and that they would have to determine his sentence if he was convicted of first-degree murder with special circumstances. The jury was death-qualified; they could impose the death penalty in an appropriate case.

To connect Catarino Gonzalez to the shooting of Officer Filbert Cuesta, the prosecution presented the testimony of eyewitnesses Agipato Negron and Sylvia Thomas, both of whom had testified at the preliminary hearing. Sylvia Thomas was an effective witness, as she positively identified the defendant as the person she saw from her balcony shooting at the police officers. However, the centerpiece of the prosecution case was the taped statements in which Gonzalez admitted shooting at the police car with the intent to scare the officers.

To help establish the shooter's real state of mind, the prosecution introduced a videotape prepared by Officer Scott Reitz, a primary firearms instructor for the Los Angeles Police Department. The videotape consisted of firing a Glock nine-millimeter handgun at a vehicle 147 feet away. (This was the distance from the shooting location to the police vehicle.) Part of the demonstration showed the recoil effect of the handgun after each shot, indicating that the shooter had to bring his arm down after each recoil and re-aim the weapon at the police car before firing the next shot. This testimony allowed prosecutor Darren Levine to argue to the jury that Catarino Gonzalez formed the intent to shoot each of the eleven times he fired in the direction of the police car.

Catarino Gonzalez testified in his own defense. He testified that he did not take a gun to the wedding reception. He was at the party when the shots were fired. When he heard the shots, he ran out the back, went through a gate and over a fence, and ran to his sister Araceli's house on Dunsmuir Avenue. Because no one was home, he entered the house through a window. Gonzalez testified that he did not shoot Officer Cuesta.

After a five-week trial, the attorneys presented their arguments to the jury. Prosecutors Darren Levine and Loni Peterson argued that the totality of the evidence clearly established that Catarino Gonzalez had shot and killed Officer Filbert Cuesta.

Defense attorney Michael Anton told the jury that his client was innocent. He argued that Gonzalez gave a false statement because of intimidation from investigators. The investigators wore down Gonzalez until he told them what they wanted to hear.

After twelve days of deliberation, the jury convicted Catarino Gonzalez of the first-degree murder of Officer Filbert Cuesta with the special circumstances that the victim was a peace officer in the performance of his duties; the murder was committed to avoid a lawful arrest; and that it was committed by means of lying in wait. Gonzalez was also convicted of the premeditated attempted murder of Officer Gabaldon.

Since the jury had found special circumstances to be true, the defendant was subject to the death penalty. The jury would decide whether he would receive a sentence of death or life without parole.

PENALTY PHASE

At the penalty phase, the prosecution introduced evidence of how the death of Officer Cuesta impacted the lives of his wife and two young daughters. Fellow officers testified to his love for his family and devotion to his job.

The defense called as witnesses several members of Catarino Gonzalez' extended family (he had five sisters and four brothers). They testified to their love and affection for him and asked the jury to spare his life.

Gonzalez' older brother, Oscar, testified that his brother's life spiraled out of control when Oscar left the family to join the Marines. He stated that in the area they lived, it was almost a given that Catarino would become a gang member without an older brother as a strong male role model.

Prosecutor Darren Levine told the jury that Catarino Gonzalez was a coldblooded, heartless assassin who should receive the death penalty for the ambush style murder of Officer Cuesta.

Defense attorney David Evans pleaded to the jurors for mercy for his client, arguing that the death penalty should be reserved for the worst of the worst, such as mass murderers and serial killers.

On June 21, 2001, the jury deliberated only three hours before returning with a recommendation of life in prison without the possibility of parole. One juror stated to reporters that there was little dissension in their deliberations during the penalty phase since Gonzalez had no prior history of violence or other circumstances to warrant the death penalty.

On September 14, 2001, Judge Robert Perry sentenced Catarino Gonzalez to the maximum penalty under the law. He was sentenced to life imprisonment without the possibility of parole, consecutive to a term of twenty-five years for using a firearm. On the attempted murder count, Gonzalez was sentenced to a consecutive term of fifteen years, consecutive to a term of twenty years to life for using a firearm.

COURT OF APPEAL OPINION

Catarino Gonzalez appealed his conviction and sentence. His main contention on appeal was that his incriminating statements were obtained in violation of the *Miranda* decision and should have been excluded. On December 19, 2003, the Second District of the Court of Appeal rendered its decision in an unpublished opinion.

The three-judge court unanimously ruled that the defendant's right to counsel was violated and that his incriminating statements were improperly admitted into evidence. Justice Paul Boland concluded the following in his written opinion:

> *"We conclude appellant adequately invoked his right to counsel at the conclusion of the first interrogation session when he said, 'if for anything you guys are going to charge me, I want to talk to a public defender, too, for any little thing.' This was a sufficiently clear articulation of a desire to speak to counsel at that time or before further question by police officers or their representatives that a reasonable police officer in the circumstances should have understood the statement to be a request for an attorney."*

The opinion further stated that the statements Gonzalez subsequently made to polygraph operator Ervin Youngblood and to Detective Aldahl were obtained in violation of *Miranda*. The trial court therefore erred in permitting the prosecution to introduce the statements in its case-in-chief at trial.

The Court of Appeal found that the erroneous admission of Gonzalez' statements contributed to the verdict. The judgment was reversed, and the case was remanded to the trial court for a new trial.

The ruling by the Court of Appeal was a devastating blow to the prosecution. It appeared the prosecution would have to retry Catarino Gonzalez for the murder of Officer Cuesta without using as evidence the incriminating statements of the defendant.

The California Attorney General's Office was handling the appeal for the People. The only appeal available to the Attorney General was to the California Supreme Court. However, the California Constitution provides no right of appeal to the California Supreme Court. Review by the Court is a matter of discretion, and only a small number of cases are granted review. Nevertheless, the Attorney General decided to file a petition for review with the California Supreme Court.

To the delight (and surprise) of the prosecution, the California Supreme Court agreed on March 24, 2004, to review the ruling of the Court of Appeal.

CALIFORNIA SUPREME COURT DECISION

On January 24, 2005, the California Supreme Court issued its opinion in the case of *People v. Catarino Gonzalez, Jr.* at 34 Cal.4th 1111 (2005). In a unanimous decision, the Supreme Court overturned the Court of Appeal ruling that had granted Gonzalez a new trial for a perceived violation of his right to counsel.

Justice Carlos Moreno wrote the opinion. He agreed with trial Judge Robert Perry that Gonzalez' statement regarding a public defender was ambiguous and that Gonzalez had sufficient experience with the police from prior arrests to understand how to invoke his right to counsel if he wished to do so.

Justice Moreno set forth the applicable law and the court's holding in the first two paragraphs of his written opinion, as follows:

> In <u>Davis v. United States</u> *(1994) 512 U.S. 452 (Davis), The United States Supreme Court held that a defendant's invocation of the right to counsel during custodial interrogation, safeguarded by* <u>Miranda v. Arizona</u> *(1966) 384 U.S. 436, must be unambiguous and unequivocal to be valid. In the present case, defendant said, before submitting to a polygraph*

examination during a custodial interrogation, "if for any-thing you guys are going to charge me, I want to talk to a public defender, too, for any little thing." The police assured him he could talk to a public defender "anytime you want to," but explained they planned to "book" him that night and would release him the following day if the polygraph examination showed he was telling the truth about his involvement in the murder that police suspected him of having committed. The interrogation continued that evening and the following day. Defendant ultimately confessed to the crime.

The Court of Appeal concluded defendant's statement was a "sufficiently clear" request for counsel and that, at a minimum, the police should have asked defendant to clarify whether he wanted an attorney. We disagree. For the reasons that follow, we conclude that defendant's statement was am-biguous and equivocal and that the police were not required to ask clarifying questions to determine his intent.

The High Court's decision reinstated Gonzalez' conviction for first-degree murder and his sentence of life in prison without the possibility of parole. Gonzalez is currently serving his sentence in the California State Prison system.

LESSONS LEARNED

It is difficult to survive a gunfire ambush by a determined attacker. Unfor-tunately, there has been an increase in ambush attacks on officers in re-cent years. Remaining vigilant to the possibility and rehearsing immediate tactical reactions can make a difference in survivability.

Officer Cuesta and his partner did the right thing when they drove away from the party location and positioned themselves to await respond-ing back-up units. The killer opened fire without warning from approximately fifty yards behind the officers, tragically resulting in Officer Cuesta's death.

The lesson to be learned from the investigation of this murder of a police officer is for detectives to be very careful about *Miranda* by clearing up the suspect's ambiguous statements that gave the defense an opening to try to suppress the suspect's statement. It is not at all clear what suspect Gonzalez meant when, during his taped interrogation, he said, "If for anything you guys are going to charge me, I want to talk to a public defender, too, for any little thing." When a suspect says something strange like that and mentions the "lawyer" word (in this case, "public defender"), it would be a good time for a detective to say something like, "Sorry, you lost me there, bro'," and see what the suspect says next. The conversation could play out many different ways, but the point is to get clarity on the record as to whether the suspect was invoking his *Miranda* rights or not.

In this case, it is fortunate the California Supreme Court ultimately ruled that the detectives did not violate *Miranda* when the suspect made an ambiguous statement about a "public defender." But that ruling came after an appellate court ruled the opposite. With appellate court and supreme court justices changing every now and then (and some appellate judges getting appointed to the Supreme Court), who knows which way the courts would rule when the issue arises again?

No doubt the Cuesta family, prosecutors, and detectives lost some sleep during the years between the murder conviction and the California Supreme Court's favorable ruling while the system pondered the suspect's ambiguous words.

COMMENTARY OF STEVE COOLEY

The decision in *Miranda v. Arizona* regarding the admissibility of confessions in criminal proceedings was handed down by the United States Supreme Court in 1966. Since then, thousands of trial courts and appellate courts have ruled on the admissibility of confessions based on the guidelines set forth in the *Miranda* opinion. Occasionally, the Supreme Court has explained and clarified the *Miranda* rules. All the courts in the United States are obligated to make their rulings regarding confessions based on the decisions of the United States Supreme Court.

As relevant to the prosecution of Catarino Gonzales, the United States Supreme Court in its 1994 decision of *Davis v. United States* held that a defendant's invocation of the right to counsel during custodial interrogation must be unambiguous and unequivocal. In this case, trial judge Robert Perry conducted a full-scale pretrial hearing and concluded that the defendant's statements regarding an attorney were ambiguous and did not amount to an "unambiguous and unequivocal" request for counsel. As a result, the defendant's confession was admissible at his trial.

It is difficult to understand how all three judges of a court of appeal could misapply the law and suppress the confession of an admitted cop killer. Fortunately, a unanimous California Supreme Court ruled that the confession was properly admitted into evidence and reinstated the defendant's conviction for first-degree murder.

Officer Filbert Henry Cuesta, Jr

Officer Filbert Cuesta with wife Sylvia and daughter Samantha, shortly before birth of daughter Sierra

Date of birth:	November 8, 1971
Date appointed:	March 21, 1994
End of watch:	August 9, 1998

Graffiti in which the word "police" had a line drawn through it, indicating the gang intended to kill a police officer

Photographs of Catarino Gonzalez at wedding reception

Victim officers' vehicle at crime scene

<<DIGITIZED COPY BA172833 Vol:GONZALEZ Seq:80178355 page:57 Printed by: 480483 on: 10/02/20
12:45 PM>>

C 133

POLICE BULLETIN

LOS ANGELES POLICE DEPARTMENT
ROBBERY-HOMICIDE DIVISION
(For Circulation Among Police Officers Exclusively)
August 10, 1998
A PUBLICATION OF THE POLICE DEPARTMENT, CITY OF LOS ANGELES, CALIFORNIA
BERNARD C. PARKS, CHIEF OF POLICE

WANTED FOR QUESTIONING IN
MURDER OF LOS ANGELES POLICE OFFICER

Catarino Gonzalez, Jr.
Monikers: "Gimo" "Termite"
5462 Smiley

M/HISP; 506; 130
DBA: 3/17/78

J# 01323032   CII A10887265

For further information, contact Det. Richard Aldahl or Det. Tom Mathews,
Robbery-Homicide Division, at (213) 485-2129. After hours, contact
Detective Headquarters Division at (213) 485-2504.

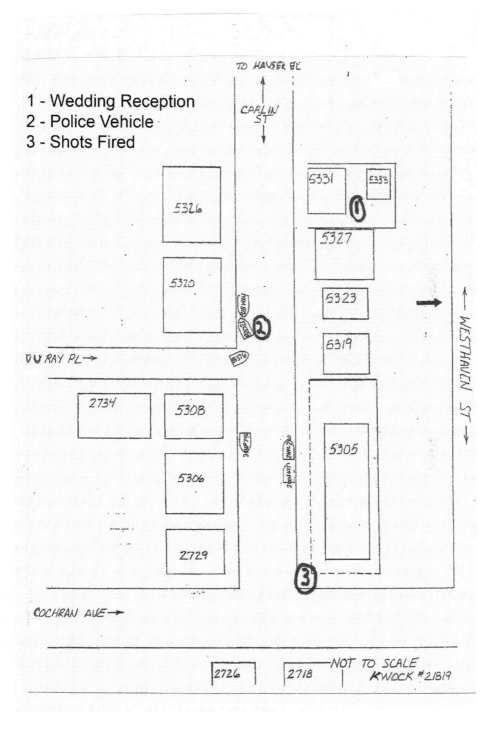

1 - Wedding Reception
2 - Police Vehicle
3 - Shots Fired

North-west corner of Cochran and Carlin street from which shots were fired

PEOPLE v. GONZALEZ   1111
34 Cal.4th 1111; 23 Cal.Rptr.3d 295; 104 P.3d 98 [Jan. 2005]

[No. S122240. Jan. 24, 2005.]

THE PEOPLE, Plaintiff and Respondent, v.
CATARINO GONZALEZ, JR., Defendant and Appellant.

SUMMARY

Defendant was convicted of first degree murder under Pen. Code, § 187, subd. (a), and premeditated attempted murder. Before submitting to a polygraph examination during a custodial interrogation, defendant made a statement about wanting an attorney if he was going to be charged. The police assured defendant that he could talk to an attorney, but the police would release him the following day if the examination showed he was telling the truth. Defendant ultimately confessed to the crime. After the jury found defendant guilty, the trial court sentenced him. (Superior Court of Los Angeles County, No. BA172833, Robert J. Perry, Judge.) The Court of Appeal, Second Dist., Div. Eight, No. B154557, reversed, finding that defendant had adequately invoked his right to counsel after having initially waived his rights. The Court of Appeal held that the police should have asked defendant to clarify whether he wanted an attorney present and that the error in admitting defendant's statement was not harmless.

The Supreme Court reversed the judgment of the Court of Appeal, holding that defendant's statement was ambiguous and equivocal and that the police were not required to ask clarifying questions to determine his intent. Defendant's statement to police was conditional, which rendered the statement ambiguous. A reasonable officer would have understood only that defendant might have been invoking the right to counsel, which was insufficient under case law to require the cessation of questioning. Defendant was given an opportunity to clarify his statement, but he failed to do so. The officers could have reasonably assumed that defendant was capable of making an unequivocal request for counsel if he so desired. Thus, the reversal of defendant's conviction was error. (Opinion by Moreno, J., expressing the unanimous view of the court.)

First page of California Supreme Court decision reinstating the defendant's conviction for first degree murder

Catarino Gonzalez holding Glock

CHAPTER SEVEN

Officer Thomas Joel Steiner

California Highway Patrol

"Sometimes the Uniform is the Target"

April 21, 2004

OFFICER THOMAS JOEL STEINER

THOMAS JOEL STEINER was born on February 14, 1969, in Sterling, Virginia, to parents Ron and Carol Steiner. The family also included daughter Julie. Ron Steiner worked for computer and telecommunication companies. In 1981, the family moved to Ohio and then in 1984 to California. They settled in the Los Altos area of Long Beach.

Tom Steiner graduated from Milliken High School in 1987 where he was a star on the baseball team. His high school sweetheart during his junior and senior years was Heidi Stephens. They lived a few houses apart, and the alphabetical listings in the high school yearbook for 1986 and 1987 put their photographs next to each other—Tom Steiner and Heidi Stephens. After high school they went in different directions. Tom Steiner worked and attended Cal Poly Pomona part time, earning a bachelor's degree in business administration in 1997. Heidi married and had a son, Justin.

Steiner joined the California Highway Patrol in October 1998. During his cadet training, he was the outstanding marksman in his class. He graduated from the CHP Academy on April 23, 1999 and was assigned to the Santa Fe Springs office upon graduation. He remained in this assignment for the next five years.

After joining the Highway Patrol, Tom Steiner crossed paths with Heidi Stephens. She was divorced and had custody of her son, Justin. Their old romance was rekindled, and they married in a private ceremony in Lake Arrowhead in 2000. In 2001 they had a son Bryan.

APRIL 21, 2004

On Wednesday April 21, 2004, shortly after 4:00 a.m., California Highway Patrol Officer Thomas Steiner left his home in Long Beach to drive to work. He arrived at the Santa Fe Springs station approximately twenty minutes later and dressed for duty. He attended the early morning briefing and then went on patrol in a one-man marked police car. He patrolled the Pomona Freeway near Diamond Bar where his primary responsibility was ticketing speeding trucks. Between 6:00 a.m. and noon, he ticketed ten truck drivers mostly for speeding, and assisted stranded motorists. After lunch, Steiner drove to the Pomona Courthouse on Mission Road. He entered the traffic court in Division One on the first floor of the courthouse where he was scheduled to testify on some traffic cases set for 1:30 p.m. His testimony was required in only one case in which he had cited the driver for following too closely. The judicial officer ruled against the driver, and Officer Steiner left the courthouse at approximately 2:45 p.m. Upon leaving the courthouse, he turned left onto Mission Road and walked south toward Seventh Street and the parking lot where his car was located for the drive home after a long day. He was wearing a blue CHP uniform, had on a bullet-proof vest, and was in possession of his service revolver.

When Officer Steiner reached Seventh Street, he apparently waited for traffic to go by before crossing the street to the parking lot. Suddenly a red car pulled up and stopped. The driver and sole occupant of the vehicle fired three shots through the driver's window at Officer Steiner. Two of the shots were deflected by his bullet-proof vest, but the third shot entered the back of his head. He fell to the ground, mortally wounded. After firing the shots from the vehicle, the driver drove off eastbound on Seventh Street.

The shooting of Officer Steiner took place in the Pomona Civic Center which contained buildings housing a number of city and county agencies. Within minutes after the shooting, numerous uniformed officers had responded to the scene including personnel from the courthouse, the Los Angeles County Sheriff's Department, the Pomona Police Department, and the Pomona Fire Department.

One of the first persons to respond was firefighter Joe Murray. He was at the fire station nearby when he heard what he believed to be multiple gunshots. He ran to the location and observed Officer Steiner lying face down on the ground. He observed wounds to the back of the victim's head and to the temple area. The victim was unresponsive. Firefighter Murray was assisted by other fire department personnel before Officer Steiner was transported by ambulance to Pomona Valley Hospital Medical Center. With his parents and wife by his side, he was pronounced dead at approximately 7:00 p.m. from a gunshot wound to the head.

Detective Gregg Guenther of the Pomona Police Department was at the station when he learned of the shooting of Officer Steiner. He had been a police officer since May 1980 and had been a homicide investigator since February 1991. During his career as a homicide investigator, he had been involved in more than 175 homicide investigations. He and his partner Tom Snyder were immediately assigned by their supervisor to conduct the investigation. They walked a short distance to the crime scene, arriving at approximately 2:58 p.m.

CRIME SCENE INVESTIGATION

The initial part of the crime scene investigation by Detectives Guenther and Snyder consisted primarily of organizing for the preservation and collection of evidence around the actual scene. They were also involved in coordinating officers to handle various duties including securing and interviewing witnesses.

There were a number of witnesses who had either observed the shooting or heard the shots fired and looked in the direction of the shooting. These witnesses observed a red vehicle with a young male driver leaving the shooting location. These witnesses were interviewed by detectives working the investigation. Below is a summary of the statements of some of the key eyewitnesses.

Corey Spencer

Corey Spencer was an eighteen-year-old student who was attending Ayala High School in Chino. He had parked his vehicle on Seventh Street and was waiting to cross the street. He saw the CHP officer standing on the north sidewalk apparently waiting for traffic to go by before crossing the street. A red car pulled up in the area and stopped. He heard four shots and observed the driver and sole occupant of the vehicle shooting a gun through the driver's side window. The shooter's right arm was extended across his body as he was shooting the gun. After the shots were fired, the vehicle quickly drove eastbound on Seventh Street toward Garey Avenue.

Spencer described the driver and sole occupant as a Hispanic male in his twenties. He stated that the vehicle was a red Acura, around 1988 model year.

Kayla Rivera

Kayla Rivera was a thirteen-year-old student at Fremont Junior High School. She was walking on Seventh Street with her friend, Maria Chadolla, when she heard several gunshots. She and Maria began to run, but she looked back and saw a red vehicle going eastbound on Seventh Street passing them. She recognized the vehicle as the same one she had seen on Park Avenue a short time before.

She described the vehicle as a medium red Acura, stock condition with no tint on the windows. She stated that she knows Acuras and had no doubt as to the make. She described the driver as a male Mexican, eighteen-to-nineteen-years-of-age, bald, and clean shaven.

Maria Chadolla gave a similar account as Kayla Rivera except that her description of the suspect vehicle was "a red car."

Ampelia Medina

Ampelia Medina, a fifty-three-year-old grandmother, was walking with her daughter and granddaughter behind the CHP officer. She heard what she thought were firecrackers and saw the officer go to the ground. She and her daughter got down also. She saw a red car going eastbound on the wrong side of the road. The car was driving past and shooting at the same time without coming to a stop. She noticed that the gun was in the driver's right hand and that he was shooting across his body. She described the vehicle as a small red car that was very clean.

Obdulia Medina

Obdulia Medina was the twenty-eight-year-old daughter of Ampelia Medina. She gave a similar account as her mother. However, she added that the suspect vehicle was an older, faded red Acura and that there was nothing special about the car.

Lourdes Mejia

Lourdes Mejia was a 37-year-old Hispanic female who was in the parking lot across the street at Seventh Street when she heard three or four rapid shots. She observed a red car with a sole occupant rapidly driving away. She stated that she could identify the vehicle if she saw it again.

Neville Tucker

Neville Tucker, a seventy-year-old male, was walking with his wife toward the courthouse when he heard three or four shots. He observed a red vehicle containing a sole occupant leaving eastbound on Seventh Street toward Garey Avenue. He stated that he was pretty sure he could identify the suspect vehicle if he saw it again.

RECOVERY OF SUSPECT VEHICLE

Several other witnesses described seeing a red car. Officers conducting a survey and search of the area located a red Acura with California license number 2TMC895 behind a flower shop at 1325 South Garey Avenue, about one mile from the scene of the shooting. Several witnesses were transported to the area to look at the vehicle. Corey Spencer and another witness were unsure if it was the correct vehicle. However, Kayla Rivera and Lourdes Mejia were positive that it was the same vehicle that left the scene of the shooting. Neville Tucker was almost sure that it was the correct vehicle.

The red 1990 Acura was registered to Valentino Arenas, an adult Hispanic male. Detectives prepared a photograph lineup containing the photo of Valentino Mitchell Arenas, the sixteen-year-old son of the registered owner of the vehicle. The photo lineup was shown to several of the witnesses, but no one was able to make a positive identification.

ARREST AND INTERROGATION

On April 22, 2004, at approximately 3:00 a.m., sixteen-year-old Valentino Mitchell Arenas was arrested by a surveillance team in the area of the 1300 block of Garey Avenue in the city of Pomona. He was transported after his arrest to the Pomona Police Department. Arenas was arrested approximately twelve hours after the shooting of Officer Thomas Steiner.

Detectives Gregg Guenther and Tom Snyder went to the Pomona Police Department to interview Valentino Arenas. The interview began at

4:53 a.m. and lasted approximately seventy-three minutes. The entire interview was videotaped with Detective Guenther doing most of the questioning. Detective Guenther read Arenas his *Miranda* rights from his *Miranda* card and asked him if he understood his rights, at which time Arenas stated, "yeah." Arenas then gave a statement fully confessing to the shooting of Officer Steiner.

Below is an excerpt from the interview in which Arenas admitted shooting the officer with a gun stolen from his grandfather and the red car stolen from his father.

GUENTHER: *Okay, when, tell us what happened. When you drove up to that officer, tell us what happened.*

ARENAS: *Basically, what you heard.*

GUENTHER: *I know, but I need you to tell me. Because I don't, I don't want to try to make, put words in your mouth. I need you to tell me 'cause all we want is the truth out of this. Just tell us what happened when you pulled up to the officer. (Pause) Once you say it I think it will be okay.*

ARENAS: *I shot him man.*

GUENTHER: *Okay, what, you did shoot him. When you, when you shot him, did you say anything to him before you shot him?*

ARENAS: *Yeah.*

GUENTHER: *What did you say to him?*

ARENAS: *My neighborhood.*

GUENTHER: *Your neighborhood, which is what?*

ARENAS: *12.*

GUENTHER:	*12. You're a mem..., you're 12th Street?*
ARENAS:	*I'm not a member though.*
GUENTHER:	*You're not a member.*
ARENAS:	*Uh un (negative).*
GUENTHER:	*Were you doing this to try to become a member?*
ARENAS:	*Something like that.*
GUENTHER:	*Okay. When you pulled up and you said "12," how many times did you shoot him or shoot at him?*
ARENAS:	*Three.*
GUENTHER:	*Three times? What kind of gun did you have?*
ARENAS:	*I stole it.*
GUENTHER:	*You stole it? What kind was it?*
ARENAS:	*About a 38.*
GUENTHER:	*38, what it look like?*
ARENAS:	*Silver.*
GUENTHER:	*Silver. How big was it?*
ARENAS:	*Like that. (describing)*
GUENTHER:	*Okay. Did... .*
ARENAS:	*(unintelligible) ...stole from my grandpa.*
GUENTHER:	*You stole it from your grandpa?*
ARENAS:	*I stole it.*
GUENTHER:	*Your grandpa on Ninth Street?*
ARENAS:	*Umm hmm. I stole it.*

GUENTHER:	Okay.
ARENAS:	And I stole my dad's car, too.
GUENTHER:	The red car?
ARENAS:	Umm hmm.

During the interview, Detective Guenther was paged and told that the apparent murder weapon had been located wrapped in a shirt under a truck near the location where Arenas had been arrested. Guenther then continued the interview with Arenas:

GUENTHER:	Can you hang on. I just got paged. [long pause] Hey, Val, they uh, the reason I stepped out is they found the gun.
ARENAS:	Um, is that right.
GUENTHER:	Yeah. Do you remember, do you remember leaving it by the truck when you got out?
ARENAS:	Sir, I just snapped, sir.
GUENTHER:	Okay. Just relax. Just relax, Val, okay. Do you remember when you got out of the car, do you remember putting it around one of the trucks, kind of hiding it?
ARENAS:	Yeah.
GUENTHER:	Where did you hide it by the truck?
ARENAS:	I wrapped it up in a shirt.
GUENTHER:	Wrapped it in a shirt?
ARENAS:	Yeah.
GUENTHER:	And where did you put it on the truck?
ARENAS:	Under it.

GUENTHER: *Under it. Okay...*

Toward the end of the interview, Detective Guenther questioned Arenas about the circumstances and randomness of the shooting.

GUENTHER: *Okay. Just a couple of more things and we'll be done. One is you mentioned that you had driven around. Once you decided you had driven around during that hour or so looking for a policeman, why is it you went by the courthouse? What made you decide to do that?*

ARENAS: *I don't know. Something just told me to go.*

GUENTHER: *Something just told you to go?*

ARENAS: *I went.*

GUENTHER: *Okay. Was there ever a point where you were close to shooting a different officer before him?*

ARENAS: *No.*

GUENTHER: *The opportunity was never there?*

ARENAS: *Maybe.*

GUENTHER: *Pardon me.*

ARENAS: *Uh un (negative).*

GUENTHER: *No. Okay, that was the first chance you had?*

ARENAS: *Yes.*

GUENTHER:	*Okay. Is uh, well, as far as that, that particular policeman, had you ever seen him before?*
ARENAS:	*No.*
GUENTHER:	*You never met him, seen him. He never stopped you. No?*
ARENAS:	*(Unintelligible)*
GUENTHER:	*Pardon me.*
ARENAS:	*Yep.*
GUENTHER:	*Yes. Okay. Was the policeman able to say anything back to you when you said "12"?*
ARENAS:	*No. Never had a chance.*
GUENTHER:	*Never had a chance?*
ARENAS:	*No.*
GUENTHER:	*When you said "12", did you just say "12" or did you say, "this is 12" or ....?*
ARENAS:	*Just 12.*
GUENTHER:	*Just 12?*
ARENAS:	*12.*
GUENTHER:	*Okay. Okay.*

Detective Guenther then asked Valentino Arenas about his reasons for shooting Officer Steiner, specifically if it was to impress 12th Street gang members.

GUENTHER:	Okay. Um, you said that you thought that shooting the policeman would be a good way to get into the gang?
ARENAS:	Yeah.
GUENTHER:	Did someone tell you that?
ARENAS:	No.
GUENTHER:	You just, that's something you thought of yourself? Nobody asked you to go out and do it?
ARENAS:	No.
GUENTHER:	And nobody asked or told you, you need to do this in order to get in the gang? Did you just know that if you did it, then that you would get in? Is that what you thought?
ARENAS:	Yeah.
GUENTHER:	Okay. How long have you been associating with 12th Street?
ARENAS:	I used to kick with some of them, but I never been associating with them.
GUENTHER:	So you thought that if you were to do this today, then you could go to them and say look what I did?
ARENAS:	Yes.
GUENTHER:	Is that the idea? Okay.

Detective Guenther concluded the interview with some clarifying questions about the gun and the car.

GUENTHER: *When you stole the car from your dad, was that from the house in Fontana or out here?*

ARENAS: *Fontana.*

GUENTHER: *Fontana. So, you stole…*

ARENAS: *I stole it.*

GUENTHER: *…the car first?*

ARENAS: *Yeah.*

GUENTHER: *And then you came down and stole the gun, or did you steal the gun first?*

ARENAS: *No. I stole the car first, and then I stole the gun.*

GUENTHER: *And then you came down, okay. So your grandpa still doesn't know you have the gun?*

ARENAS: *No.*

GUENTHER: *All right. And what's your grandpa's name?*

ARENAS: *Val. Valentino Arenas.*

GUENTHER: *Okay. How old is he?*

ARENAS: *Sixty-something.*

GUENTHER: *Okay. Okay. That about does it. I tell you what, Val, obviously we need, we have to take you down to our jail now, okay.*

ARENAS: *Let's go.*

POST-CONFESSION STATEMENT

After his taped confession, Valentino Arenas was processed by officers at the Pomona Police Department. At approximately 6:00 a.m., in front of four witnesses, Arenas was in the print room of the jail when he became very nervous and appeared to panic. He spontaneously stated that he did not kill that cop and knew for a fact that he missed the officer. He then stated that the bullets passed between the officer's arm, although he did observe one round strike the officer in the shoulder. Arenas was very animated and demonstrated with his hands the direction in which the bullets traveled. He stated that if he wanted to kill the cop, he could have with no problem. He wanted to speak to the detective who interviewed him earlier. [Note: Detectives Guenther and Snyder did not return for another interview.]

RECOVERY OF MURDER WEAPON

At approximately 5:00 a.m. on the early morning of April 22, 2004, a handgun was located under a small delivery truck that was parked in the side parking lot of the business at 1325 South Garey Avenue. This was close to the location where the red Acura was parked and where Arenas had been arrested.

The weapon was a chrome five shot Charter Arms "Off Duty .38 SPL" revolver bearing serial number 886754. The revolver contained five G.F.L. caliber spent cartridge casings, all five bullets had been fired. The weapon was wrapped in a blue "Dickies" shirt.

Valentino Arenas, the grandfather of the suspect Valentino Arenas, III, identified the revolver as having been stolen from his residence. The revolver, the five cartridge casings, a bullet fragment, and a deformed bullet recovered from Officer Steiner's brain during the autopsy were submitted to an expert firearms examiner for analysis. He determined that the bullet fragment and deformed bullet were fired from the revolver and the five expended cartridge cases were from the revolver.

EVENTS AFTER DEATH OF OFFICER STEINER

The investigation into the death of Officer Thomas Steiner moved rapidly. In less than twenty-four hours after his death, the following had occurred:

1. The crime scene was preserved, and evidence was recovered.

2. Numerous witnesses were interviewed.

3. Valentino Arenas was arrested and gave a taped confession.

4. The vehicle and the gun used were recovered.

5. An autopsy was performed on the body of Officer Steiner on the morning of April 22, 2004. The autopsy ascribed the cause of death to a gunshot wound to the head. The bullet had entered the back of the victim's head and lodged in his brain. The bullet was deformed with a small area fragmented and missing from the projectile recovered from the brain. That missing fragment exited through the head of the victim.

On April 23, the District Attorney's Crimes Against Police Officers Section (CAPOS) filed murder charges against Valentino Mitchell Arenas, III. Even though Arenas was sixteen-years-of-age, the case was filed in adult court because of the serious nature of the crime. The charges consisted of one count of first-degree murder with gun use and criminal street gang allegations. Three special circumstance allegations were alleged: the victim was a police officer engaged in the performance of his duties, the victim was killed by means of lying in wait, and the murder was perpetrated by means of discharging a firearm from a motor vehicle. Because he was a juvenile, Arenas was not eligible for the death penalty. His maximum penalty was life imprisonment without the possibility of parole.

"THE ULTIMATE HATE CRIME"

On April 22, 2004, I issued a statement that "This was the ultimate hate crime--the random assassination of a law enforcement officer based solely on the victim's status in the community and a uniform worn. Those who commit these crimes and those who aid, abet and encourage the cowardly gang subculture should be condemned."

I also announced that Valentino Arenas would be charged as an adult with the murder of a peace officer. Arenas could not receive the death penalty due to his age. I stated that the District Attorney's Office would seek the most severe sentence possible, life imprisonment without the possibility of parole.

California Governor Arnold Schwarzenegger ordered Capitol flags be flown at half-staff in honor of the slain officer. In a statement, the Governor said, "Thomas was a true hero and a valiant police officer who spent the last five years of his life protecting the lives of others. It is a tragedy to lose Thomas in the line of duty. Maria and I offer our condolences to his family and friends during this difficult time."

Officer Thomas Steiner was universally praised by his co-workers in the California Highway Patrol. He was described as a friendly and dedicated police officer who loved his job and his family.

BURIAL OF OFFICER THOMAS STEINER

On the morning of Tuesday, April 27, I was one of more than 2,000 mourners who gathered at the Calvary Chapel in Downey to pay their final respects to Officer Thomas Steiner. California Highway Patrol Commissioner D. O. "Spike" Helmick gave an emotional eulogy, declaring, "The death of Tom Steiner has reached a new low in our history. On that date a despicable little coward murdered Tom in cold blood. I have a promise to make to all of the coward's friends: their day of reckoning is coming, and it is coming very quickly. Such cowardly acts will not be tolerated in the State of California."

12TH STREET GANG

In April 2004, the 12th Street gang was one of at least fifteen gangs in the city of Pomona. They claimed much of south Pomona, which included the civic center and courthouse where Officer Thomas Steiner was gunned down on April 21, as their turf. The 12th Street gang claimed about 1,000 members and associates and had close ties to the Mexican Mafia, one of California's most powerful prison gangs. It used the shark as its symbol, and the members were known as "Sharkies."

On May 3, 2004, two weeks after the death of Officer Steiner, 450 officers from two dozen law enforcement agencies conducted 140 raids and arrested 49 people, the majority of them 12th Street gang members. Most of the forty-nine arrests were for violations of probation or parole including associating with gang members and possession of drugs or weapons.

California Highway Patrol Commissioner D. O. "Spike" Helmick had promised a "day of reckoning" for the 12th Street gang at Steiner's funeral and said that the raid would not be the last. He stated, "We were careful and very specific in that we arrested people who had warrants for violating the law. I hope today we sent a subtle message that our state is better than this and that we will continue to do this [target gangs] until this type of behavior ceases."

PRE-TRIAL PROCEEDINGS
Preliminary Hearing

The preliminary hearing was conducted on July 8, 2004, before Judge Charles Horan of the Pomona Superior Court. Deputy District Attorney Linda Loftfield of CAPOS was the prosecutor, and defense attorney Joseph Borges represented the defendant, Valentino Arenas, III. The preliminary hearing lasted less than a half-day as prosecutor Loftfield called just two witnesses. The first witness was a gang expert who gave his expert opinion that the murder of Officer Steiner was for the benefit of the 12th Street gang. He satisfied the gang allegation alleged in the pleading documents. The second witness was Detective Gregg Guenther who testified to the hearsay statement of witness Corey Spencer and to the defendant's taped confession. Defense attorney Borges did not contest Judge Horan's finding that the evidence was sufficient to bind the defendant for trial.

Change of Venue

The case was set for trial in the Pomona Courthouse. In pre-trial proceedings before Judge Charles Horan on August 24, 2004, defense attorney Joseph Borges argued that it would be inappropriate to try the case in the Pomona Courthouse because the crime scene was right outside. Jurors would be walking by the crime scene whenever they entered the courthouse. Judge Horan agreed this could be a problem, so he transferred the trial to the Citrus Courthouse in West Covina, about eleven miles away.

Confession

Defense attorney Borges made a motion to suppress the defendant's confession that was heard before Judge Thomas Falls on November 18, 19 and 22, 2004. Arenas' confession was on tape. It clearly showed that Arenas was given and waived his *Miranda* rights and the confession was voluntarily made. Judge Falls denied the defense motion and ruled that the jury would hear the defendant's confession.

GUILTY PLEA

On December 6, 2004, jury selection was about to begin in the case against Valentino Arenas for the murder of Officer Thomas Steiner. Judge Philip Gutierrez was the trial judge in the Citrus Courthouse in West Covina. There was little doubt that Arenas would be convicted since the prosecution had an outright, or "deadbang," case. Arenas and his attorney were hoping the prosecution would allow his client to plead guilty to something less than the maximum sentence of life without the possibility of parole. However, the prosecution was holding firm that Arenas should receive the maximum sentence for his cold-blooded murder of Officer Steiner. Just before jury selection was to begin, Valentino Arenas pleaded guilty to first-degree murder and admitted the street gang, gun use, and special circumstance allegations. He was facing a sentence of life imprisonment without the possibility of parole. The date of sentencing was continued to March 10, 2005.

SENTENCING

On March 10, 2005, Valentino Mitchell Arenas, III, appeared before Los Angeles County Superior Court Judge Philip Gutierrez for sentencing. Before Judge Gutierrez imposed sentence, family members of the victim and of the defendant, as well as members of law enforcement, addressed the court.

A tearful and angry Heidi Steiner called her husband's killer an "ignorant coward" and asked the judge to send him to prison for life. She stated, "My family needs this part of the nightmare to end today. We need the peace of mind to know he will spend the rest of his life behind bars." At one point, she faced Arenas and told him, "Valentino, I don't know if you can hear or even care, but what you have done is unforgivable." She explained how her three-year-old son Bryan got excited when he saw his father's truck parked in the driveway; the boy asked if his father had come back from heaven.

After completing her statement, Heidi Steiner played a video compilation of footage filmed of her husband to the tune of "Just the Two of Us" playing in the background. Several scenes depicted Tom Steiner acting playfully with his son. One scene that brought tears to many courtroom spectators showed a playful Bryan, wearing blue sunglasses and holding an empty pitcher, telling his father, "You're the baby and I am the dad."

Ronald and Carol Steiner, the parents of Thomas Steiner, described the experiences their grandson would be unable to share with his father. Carol Steiner told the court, "No mercy was given to my son and no mercy should be given by this court."

California Highway Patrol Captain Sharon Baker stated, "In this case, there's no training that could have saved him. There's no tactical mistakes. This was not an enforcement stop. This was not a case where our guard was down."

Hoping the judge would impose a sentence making Arenas eligible for parole, his relatives took the stand and portrayed him as a boy whose father was the reason for his son's drug use and criminal behavior. Valentino Arenas, Jr., stated he and his son used methamphetamine for several days leading up to the shooting. Arenas, Jr., had been to prison for bank robbery and admitted that much of his criminal behavior was related to drug use.

Deputy District Attorney Linda Loftfield pointed out that the defendant's behavior wasn't entirely the result of his father's influence. He had been using drugs a year before his father was last paroled. Loftfield argued that Arenas had to commit a series of deliberate acts leading up to the shooting. He stole his grandfather's gun, took his father's car without permission, and drove around looking for a police officer to shoot. Loftfield stated that if he was using methamphetamine on the day of the shooting, it was to gain the courage to do the act.

There were approximately thirty uniformed CHP officers in the courtroom wearing black bands across their badges.

At the conclusion of the day's proceedings, Judge Philip Gutierrez sentenced Valentino Arenas to life in prison without the possibility of parole. He added an additional sentence of twenty-five years to life for the use of a firearm.

LESSONS LEARNED

The murder of CHP Officer Thomas Steiner was an unprovoked, cowardly act that fits the definition of "surprise attack." There is little an officer can do to protect him/herself in a situation like this, where the fatal attack is rapid and there is no opportunity to implement self-defense measures. Situational awareness and the knowledge that unprovoked ambush attacks against officers are increasing are important mind-sets. However, there are no obvious tactical lessons from this tragedy.

Thomas Steiner
CHP

Date of birth: February 14, 1969
Date appointed: October 19, 1998
End of watch: April 21, 2004

Location where Officer Steiner was shot

Aerial view of Pomona courthouse where Officer Steiner was shot

Car from which Valentino Arenas shot Officer Steiner

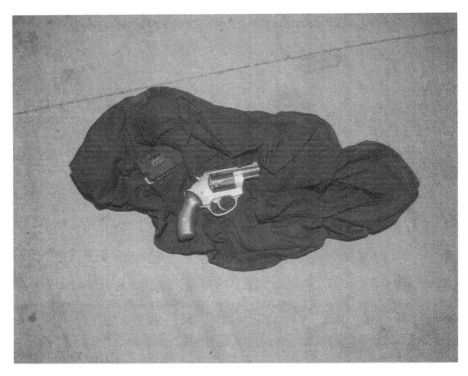

Murder weapon recovered near location where suspect was arrested

Valentino Arenas in court

CHAPTER EIGHT

Deputy Jerry Ortiz

L.A. County Sheriff's Department

"Going it Alone"

June 24, 2005

THE SHOOTING OF JEFFREY WILLIAMS

ON JUNE 20, 2005, AT APPROXIMATELY 3:00 P.M., Jeffrey Williams, an African-American man, was doing yard work in front of the house at 22418 Joliet Street in Hawaiian Gardens. Williams had been working there for a couple of weeks doing repairs on the house for the owner. Williams was a former member of the Los Angeles Bloods gang and an ex-convict. He was somewhat apprehensive about working in the area because he knew how the Hispanic Hawaiian Gardens gang felt about African-Americans.

Jose Luis Orozco drove up, approached Williams, and asked him if he wanted to buy "speed," otherwise known as methamphetamine. Williams declined, telling Orozco that he "didn't mess with it," and turned away. Williams glanced back and saw a .38-caliber revolver in Orozco's hand. Williams hit Orozco's hand, and a shot was fired. Williams ran off, and Orozco fired a shot which hit Williams in the buttocks. Williams scaled a gate as he was hit with another shot in the upper back. He made it into an adjacent backyard.

Neighbors called the police, and Williams was taken to the hospital. On the advice of doctors, he elected not to have the bullets removed. Los Angeles County Sheriff's Deputy Mark Brooks was assigned to investigate the Williams shooting. He visited Williams at the hospital and showed him a photographic lineup. Williams unequivocally identified Jose Luis Orozco's photograph, telling Deputy Brooks, "That's the son of a bitch who shot me."

ENTER DEPUTY JERRY ORTIZ

On June 23, 2005, at approximately 2:00 p.m., Deputy Mark Brooks had a conversation with Deputy Jerry Ortiz outside the Lakewood Sheriff's Station, just as Deputy Ortiz was coming on duty. Deputy Brooks and Deputy Ortiz were both gang enforcement officers with Operation Safe Streets, the Sheriff's gang suppression unit.

Deputy Jerry Ortiz was thirty-five-years-of-age and had joined the Sheriff's Department in February 1990. He was born on September 16, 1969, and raised in the Los Angeles area, where he attended El Monte High School. After high school, he joined the United States Army. After his discharge from the Army, he joined the Sheriff's Department at the age of twenty. While working as a patrol officer, he became interested in the gang problem. He joined Operation Safe Streets in 2001 after passing a background check and written exam that tested his knowledge of gang culture. Deputy Ortiz won numerous commendations for his work. In 2004, he was awarded the City of Lakewood's Medal of Valor after he fatally shot a carjacker who drew a gun on him and his partner.

Deputy Brooks told Deputy Ortiz about the Williams shooting and his suspicion that Jose Luis Orozco was involved. He told Deputy Ortiz that Orozco was a member of the Varrio Hawaiian Gardens (VHG) gang and was wanted as a parolee-at-large. He provided Deputy Ortiz with a copy of the arrest warrant for Orozco and a photograph of him. Deputy Ortiz stated that he would assist in locating Orozco.

On the evening of June 23, 2005, Jerry Ortiz told his wife, Graciela "Chela" Ortiz, that he was going out the next day to look for a parolee-at-large who had shot a black man. Deputy Ortiz told her that the person he was looking for was named "Sepe" and had horns tattooed on his forehead.

THE MURDER OF DEPUTY JERRY ORTIZ

Deputy Jerry Ortiz arrived early at work on Friday afternoon, June 24, 2005. He was usually partnered with one of two deputies, but both had the day off. Instead, Ortiz had planned to partner with his sergeant. However, he decided to go out on his own to visit a location that Jose Luis Orozco was known to frequent. He drove his patrol car to the area of the 12000 block of East 223rd Street in Hawaiian Gardens.

At approximately 3:00 p.m., Deputy Ortiz spotted Orozco, who ran toward a multi-unit apartment complex on East 223rd Street. The apartment complex consisted of two separate buildings. The front building at 12215 East 223rd Street consisted of a single bedroom apartment rented by Angela Negrete who lived there with her three young daughters; Nevaeh was an infant, Jasmine was age six, and Angelica was age seven.

The rear building at 12217 East 223rd Street consisted of four apartments. Sandra Ceballos lived in one of the apartments. Earlier in the day, she was having a problem with a clogged drain, and Orozco was at her apartment helping her with it.

In the afternoon, Priscilla Carrero and her boyfriend, Manual Aguilar, were temporarily staying at Negrete's apartment in the living room. Angela Negrete and her two older daughters were also in the living room. Shortly before 3:00 p.m., Sandra Ceballos came to Negrete's apartment to hang around.

A few minutes after Ceballos arrived, Jose Luis Orozco ran into the front house through the front door and into the living room. Angela Negrete asked Orozco what he was doing there and told him to leave. He told Negrete to keep quiet, and he put his hand over her mouth, saying "shhh."

About a minute later, Deputy Ortiz knocked on the screened security door of the front house. Negrete opened the security door and asked if she could help him. Deputy Ortiz asked her if anyone had run into her house. She lied and said, "no."

Negrete then asked Ceballos, Aguilar, and Carrero if they had seen anyone run in. They all lied by responding in the negative. Carrero and Aguilar came to the door and spoke to Deputy Ortiz. He asked to see Aguilar's identification. Aguilar produced a driver's license and handed it to Deputy Ortiz, who had stepped slightly over the threshold to receive it. Deputy Ortiz then stepped back out of the front door area with the identification in his hand.

At this time, Orozco was hiding behind the solid interior front door. He was armed with a black revolver with a brown handle. He fired one shot at Deputy Ortiz through the crack between the door and jamb, striking him in the head. Deputy Ortiz fell to the ground on his back by the front door of the residence, fatally wounded.

Negrete, her daughters, Ceballos, Aguilar, and Carrero ran out the back door to Ceballos' adjacent apartment. Orozco ran to the adjacent alley and then ran north.

WIRETAP APPLICATION

As was my habit in cases involving the murder of a police officer, I went to the crime scene. Deputy District Attorney John Nantroup of CAPOS was already there to provide legal assistance to the Sheriff's Department in its investigation. Sheriff's investigators had interviewed witnesses who had observed the shooting and determined that Jose Luis Orozco had shot and killed Deputy Jerry Ortiz.

Investigators had also determined that members of Orozco's family lived in Las Vegas. Investigators believed that Orozco may have fled to Las Vegas or may contact his family members who lived there. It is my belief that every investigative lead should be pursued in a case involving the murder of a police officer. Toward that end, members of the District Attorney's Major Narcotics Division were contacted to assist Sheriff's investigators in obtaining an emergency wiretap order for the telephones at the residence of Orozco's family in Las Vegas. Since the telephones were located in Las Vegas, the wiretap order would have to be issued by a Nevada judge. Efforts were hindered because Nevada authorities did not have experience or personnel to prepare wiretaps.

While this effort was ongoing, Orozco was arrested by a Sheriff's SWAT team hiding in a residence near the crime scene. The wiretap was no longer necessary, and the attempt to obtain one was abandoned.

RESPONSE TO MURDER SCENE

On June 24, 2005, at 3:14 p.m., 911 received the first call regarding the shooting. Los Angeles County Sheriff's Deputy Robert Spracher was the first officer to respond to the scene followed shortly thereafter by Deputy Matthew Garfin. They found Deputy Ortiz lying on his back on the ground in front of the residence with his feet toward the front door and a driver's license at his fingertips. Deputy Ortiz's gun was holstered and secured with a strap. He was wearing a bullet-proof vest over his green nylon wind-breaker; the vest had the word "Sheriff" printed in bold gold letters on the back and on the breast.

Deputy Garfin checked for a pulse but could not find one. The deputies picked up Deputy Ortiz and carried him to the street behind Deputy Garfin's patrol car. Deputy Garfin removed Deputy Ortiz's vest and administered CPR. Deputy Ortiz was transported to Tri-City Hospital in Hawaiian Gardens. CPR was continued during transport, but there were no visible signs of life.

On June 25, 2005, an autopsy was performed on the body of Jerry Ortiz by Senior Medical Examiner William Sherry. The cause of death was a gunshot wound to the head. The entrance wound was behind the left ear, and the bullet traveled through the head and rested behind the right ear. The bullet was recovered during the autopsy and given to investigating officers.

ARREST OF JOSE LUIS OROZCO

The Los Angeles County Sheriff's SWAT Team responded to the scene approximately thirty minutes after the shooting and began to set up a containment of the area to prevent persons from leaving the perimeter. Canine units searched the area, and search warrants were obtained for the front apartment and the other four apartments at the crime scene.

Cheri Willett was the mother of Jermie and Jeff Hookey; they lived at 11239 East 223rd Street, five residences from the crime scene. She heard the commotion outside her residence. She went in and out of her residence several times. On one occasion she reentered her home and observed Jose Orozco in Jermie's bedroom. She knew Orozco since he was acquainted with her sons. She asked him if he had anything to do with the shooting, but she did not hear his response. Orozco then showed her a gun with a dark muzzle and wood handle, wrapped in a shirt. Willett did not see Orozco leave her residence.

Sometime around midnight, investigators served a search warrant for Cheri Willett's residence and garage. The search warrant was served by SWAT Team members and canine officers. Jose Luis Orozco was located in the bathtub, which was filled with wet towels. He was unarmed and was arrested without incident. Apparently, he was hiding in the bathtub, so he could use the wet towels to protect his eyes in case tear gas was used.

During the search of Willett's residence, a .38 caliber Taurus revolver with a brown wooden grip was found in the living room in a cardboard box containing stereo equipment. The maximum capacity of the cylinder was five rounds; the revolver contained five rounds in the cylinder. Ballistics tests determined that this was the gun that fired the bullet into the head of Deputy Ortiz. DNA samples collected from the hammer, muzzle, trigger, interior and exterior handle of the gun all matched Orozco's DNA.

THE BELLFLOWER JAIL CONVERSATION

On the afternoon of July 8, 2005, Jose Luis Orozco, Jermie Hookey, and Victor Vasquez were together in the Bellflower jail lockup. The three individuals were members of the Varrio Hawaiian Gardens gang. Their conversation was surreptitiously recorded. During the conversation, they discussed the murder of Deputy Ortiz. Orozco stated that the police found the gun in the surround-sound box in the living room "where Hookey's sound shit was." Orozco mentioned the police did not have the shell casing, and Hookey confirmed that he had "flushed it."

In response to a question from Vasquez about whether police found gunpowder on his arms, Orozco stated, "I pissed on my hands."

Orozco expressed concern that Angela Negrete was cooperating with the police. Hookey and Orozco agreed that something had to be done about Angela. Hookey stated Vasquez was getting out and that "he knows what to do. Put the word on the street." Orozco told Vasquez to "let Maniac know." They agreed that if they couldn't find Angela because she was in protective custody, they would start taking family and "put them in an early grave."

HISTORY OF THE CASE PRIOR TO TRIAL
July 26, 2005

A four-count complaint against Jose Luis Orozco was filed in Los Angeles County Superior Court charging him with one count of first-degree murder (count one), one count of attempted first-degree murder (count three), and two counts of possession of a firearm by a felon (counts two and four). The complaint also included armed allegations, gang allegations, and three special circumstances that made the defendant eligible for the death penalty.

Deputy District Attorney Lowell Anger, assisted by Deputy District Attorney Phillip Stirling, both assigned to CAPOS, were selected to prosecute the case.

March 7, 2006

After a preliminary hearing, Jose Luis Orozco was held to answer on all four counts.

March 22, 2006

A four-count information signed by Deputy District Attorney Lowell Anger was filed in the Los Angeles Superior Court charging Orozco with the same crimes, armed allegations, gang allegations, and special circumstances as the complaint. The information added that Orozco had suffered two prior prison terms. Orozco pleaded not guilty to all counts and denied the allegations.

March 8, 2007

Jury selection began in the courtroom of Judge Philip Hickok in the Norwalk courthouse in late February 2007. On March 8, 2007, a twelve-person jury and six alternates were sworn.

The following is a summary of the main principals in the case and the charges against the defendant.

PEOPLE v. JOSE LUIS OROZCO
Case VA089897

JUDGE:	The Honorable Philip H. Hickok
PROSECUTORS:	Lowell Anger, Deputy District Attorney
	Phillip Stirling, Deputy District Attorney
	Crimes Against Peace Officers Section (CAPOS)
DEFENSE ATTORNEYS:	Stan Perlo, Court-appointed defense attorney

Robin Yanes, Court-appointed de-fense attorney

CHARGES:

Count I -- Murder of Deputy Luis Gerardo "Jerry" Ortiz

- Special circumstance of murder of a peace officer in the perfor-mance of his duties
- Special circumstance of murder by means of lying in wait
- Special circumstance of murder to avoid or prevent a lawful arrest

Count II -- Possession of firearm by convicted felon

Count III -- Attempted murder of Jeffrey Williams

Count IV -- Possession of firearm by convicted felon

LOCATION:

Los Angeles Superior Court
Norwalk Courthouse, Department R

GUILT PHASE OF THE TRIAL

On March 9, 2007, the prosecution commenced the presentation of its case-in-chief and called twenty-nine witnesses over the next five days of trial. The evidence covered the following areas:

1. *The attempted murder of Jeffrey Williams.* Jose Luis Orozco was positively identified by Jeffrey Williams as the person who shot him on June 24, 2005.

2. *Eyewitnesses to the murder of Deputy Jerry Ortiz.* Hawaiian Gardens is a small city. Many of the eyewitnesses were al-

ready familiar with Jose Orozco, a gang member who often frequented the area of the shooting and went by the moniker of "Sepe." He was easily identifiable by the horns tattooed on his forehead.

Angela Negrete, Sandy Ceballos, Priscilla Carrero, and Negrete's two eldest daughters were in Negrete's apartment when Orozco fired the shot that killed Deputy Ortiz. They each testified at the trial and identified Orozco either as the shooter or the person hiding behind the front door when the shot was fired.

Perhaps the most compelling testimony came from Jasmine Negrete, the seven-year-old daughter of Angela Negrete and the youngest witness in the case. Homicide Detective Dawn Retzloff led her by the hand to the witness stand. In her other hand she held a gray raccoon stuffed animal that she placed on the witness stand facing the attorneys and the audience.

Jasmine testified that on June 24, 2005, when she was six, she was at home on the carpet in her apartment. Also present were her mother, her older sister Angie, Sandra, Manuel, and Manuel's girlfriend. The defendant, whom she referred to as Sepe, was also inside the apartment. When the deputy came to the door, her mother opened the front door and talked to the deputy as Sepe hid on the other side of the front door. Sepe shot the deputy through the hinged opening of the door with a black gun that he took out of his pocket. Everyone then ran from the apartment to Sandra's house.

Several neighbors also observed Orozco at or near the shooting scene and identified him in court.

3. *The arrest of Jose Orozco and the recovery of the murder weapon.* Evidence was introduced of the arrest of the defendant hiding in the bathtub of the residence of Cheri Wil-

lett and the recovery of the murder weapon from a cardboard box in the living room.

4. *The Bellflower jail conversations.* The prosecution presented evidence of the recorded conversation among Jose Orozco, Jermie Hookey, and Victor Vasquez in the Bellflower jail lockup on July 8, 2005. During the conversation they discussed the murder of Deputy Ortiz and eliminating witnesses against Orozco.

5. *Prior Statements by Orozco about murdering police officers.* Gilbert Loeza testified that in November 2002, he had a conversation with Jose Orozco who stated that "whenever he got confronted with a cop, he's going to go balls out and shoot him." Joe Esquivel testified that in November 2005, Orozco told him that he wanted to go to Las Vegas because if he stayed in California he would wind up killing a cop.

6. *Forensic evidence.* The following forensic evidence was introduced by the prosecution during the guilt phase of the defendant's trial:
   a. A criminalist examined the door from Angela Negrete's apartment and confirmed that a gun was fired through the door jamb.
   b. A ballistics analysis confirmed that the .38 caliber gun found in the living room of the Willett residence fired the bullet taken from the head of Deputy Ortiz during the autopsy.
   c. DNA taken from the .38 caliber gun matched the DNA of Jose Orozco.

7. *Gang evidence.* Los Angeles Sheriff's Department Detective Brandt House testified as an expert on the Varrio Hawaiian Gardens (VHG) gang. At the time of the trial, VHG was comprised of approximately 800 documented members and 300 documented affiliates. The primary activities of the

gang included theft offenses, assaultive conduct including shooting at inhabited dwellings and murder, narcotics offenses, witness intimidation, and hate crimes against African Americans.

Jose Luis Orozco was a documented, self-admitted member of the VHG gang and went by the names "Sepe" and "Shyboy." He had various tattoos signifying allegiance to the gang and to the Mexican Mafia. Prior to the murder of Deputy Ortiz, Orozco lived in the garage of Cheri Willett, the mother of Jermie Hookey, a known VHG affiliate. Inside the garage, investigators found a large amount of VHG gang graffiti. Further, the walls of the Men's Central Jail where Orozco was housed prior to trial contained gang graffiti.

Detective House further testified that the effect of Deputy Ortiz's murder "makes this gang more feared than they ever were. Not just by citizens, but also [by] other gang members from opposing gangs. . . . Because the killing of a peace officer is the ultimate act that a gang member can commit, as far as peace officers are their main enemies. If they kill a peace officer, they obviously will have no qualms about killing anyone else, and it creates a serious fear in the community." (14 Reporters Transcript, page 2010.)

As for Jose Orozco, the shooting of Deputy Ortiz would significantly increase his own status within the VHG gang and among opposing gang members.

DEFENSE EVIDENCE AT GUILT PHASE AND CLOSING ARGUMENT

On Friday, March 16, 2007, the prosecution completed the presentation of its case-in-chief.

The defense faced a dilemma on how to proceed. The prosecution had presented a powerful case establishing the guilt of the defendant, and a conviction of the criminal charges against him appeared to be a virtual certainty. There appeared to be no viable defense to the charges. Under these circumstances, the defense adopted the strategy that it would concede the guilt of the defendant on the criminal charges and direct their efforts to saving their client from the death penalty.

The defense rested without calling any witnesses. Deputy District Attorney Lowell Anger presented the prosecution's closing argument, after which it was the defense's turn to present its closing argument. Defense attorney Robin Yanes then stated the following to the court and jury:

> *"Your Honor, ladies and gentlemen of the jury, the defense waives closing argument."*

Judge Philip Hickok sent the jury to the jury room and conducted the following proceedings in open court out of the presence of the jury:

COURT:	*Okay. Just to make a record of this, Mr. Yanes, have you talked to your client about waiving your argument?*
MR. YANES:	*Mr. Perlo has, your honor.* *(Defendant and his counsel confer <u>sotto voce</u>.)*
MR. PERLO:	*We've discussed that issue and the possibility that we would make an argument or not make an argument; is that correct?*
DEFENDANT:	*Yes*
COURT:	*Okay. Then knowing full well what that means, do you go ahead and concur with your attorneys' not making an argument in this case?*

DEFENDANT: *Yes*

COURT: *Okay. I'll accept that. I'll go ahead and bring
                the jury back out, give them the concluding
                instructions and I'll let them begin the delib-
                erations. Buzz the jury.*

On Monday, March 19, 2007, at 2:40 p.m., the jury began deliberations. The next day, on March 20, 2007, at 12:40 p.m., the jury returned
guilty verdicts on all counts and allegations:

Jose Luis Orozco was found guilty of the first-degree murder of Deputy Luis Gerardo "Jerry" Ortiz in count one; the attempted willful, deliberate murder of Jeffrey Williams in count three; two counts of possession
of a firearm by a felon with priors in counts two and four. The jury also
found true the special circumstance allegations: that Orozco murdered
Deputy Ortiz while the deputy was engaged in the performance of his duties, Orozco did so while lying in wait, and Orozco murdered Deputy
Ortiz to avoid and prevent a lawful arrest. Finally, the jury found true all
of the charged firearm and gang enhancement allegations.

The true findings on the special circumstances made the defendant
eligible for the death penalty. The jury was ordered to return on March 27,
2007, for the penalty phase of the trial.

PENALTY PHASE – PROSECUTION CASE

Under the California death penalty statute, there are three factors in aggravation that the prosecution may introduce at the penalty phase of a
capital case: Factor A includes the circumstances of the crime; Factor B is
prior violent criminal activity of the defendant; and Factor C is prior felony convictions.

On March 27, 2007, the penalty phase commenced. Over the next
two days the prosecution presented testimony on Factors A and B.

Factor A – the circumstances of the crime

The jury had already heard the evidence of the ambush-murder of Deputy Ortiz at the guilt phase of the trial, and they could consider that evidence at the penalty phase.

The United States Supreme Court has ruled that in determining sentence in a capital case, the jury may consider the circumstances of the crime. That includes the pain and suffering experienced by family and friends from the death of the victim. *Payne v. Tennessee* (1991) 501 U.S. 808. The prosecution introduced this victim-impact testimony from six witnesses, as follows:

1. Rosa Ortiz, the mother of Deputy Jerry Ortiz. He was the middle child of five children. He was a good athlete and enjoyed sports, especially baseball. He joined the army after high school and, after his discharge, joined the Los Angeles County Sheriff's Department.

   Jerry Ortiz's father had an infection in his leg at the time his son was murdered. After the murder, he lost the will to live and refused to take his medications. As a result, both of his legs were amputated.

2. Jeremy Ortiz was the eldest son of Jerry Ortiz from his first marriage. He was in high school at the time of the trial. Jeremy played sports with his father, and they went to sporting events together. He was the best man at his father's recent wedding to Chela. His father loved Chela, and they were very happy together.

3. Claudia Santa Anna was the sister of Deputy Jerry Ortiz. He was her best friend, and they talked every day. He escorted her when she was homecoming princess. He was a great uncle to her children, including godfather to her daughter Julianna. Julianna was baptized by Ortiz and was the daughter Ortiz would never have. He influenced her father Mondo

and their nephew Mar to become police officers. During her testimony she described various photographs depicting Jerry Ortiz with family and friends.

4. Chela Ortiz was the widow of Jerry Ortiz. They knew each other from high school and reconnected at a barbecue in 2003. They got engaged on February 15, 2005, and were married on May 28, 2005, just three weeks before his murder. Although he was a police officer and a boxer on the Sheriff's team and looked tough, he was very sensitive. He loved kids and was especially close to his nephews and nieces. She and Jerry were very much in love and planned to have children right away and grow old together.

5. Gary Gerlach was a Sheriff's deputy and the best friend of Jerry Ortiz. They were partners for two years. He was a groomsman at Ortiz's marriage to Chela and gave the eulogy at his funeral in front of 6,000 people. Ortiz was a great cop who went out of his way to help juveniles stay on the right track. He was on the Sheriff's boxing team and knew Sheriff Sherman Block. He had many close friends and made friends easily.

6. Sally Brown was an FBI agent who was investigating a public corruption case in the Long Beach Police Department. Deputy Jerry Ortiz introduced her to an informant who enabled her and her partner to build a case against a corrupt cop. The officer was convicted and sentenced to eleven years in federal prison. Ortiz received commendations from both the FBI and the Long Beach Police Department.

Factor B – prior violent criminal activity

1. Saul Camarena testified that on October 11, 2002, he was driving through Hawaiian Gardens when Jose Orozco stopped him. Orozco punched Camarena through the window. When Camarena got out of the car, Orozco pulled out a gun and hit him in the eye. Orozco told Camarena that he was going to kill him, chambered a bullet, and attempted to pull the trigger. However, Orozco's sister stopped him. Camarena refused to prosecute because he lived in the same neighborhood as Orozco and did not "want family problems."

2. Gilbert Loeza testified that on October 19, 2002, he was stabbed by Jose Orozco. He had been told that Orozco had taken the stereo out of his car, so Loeza went to Orozco's house to retrieve it. When Loeza arrived, he saw Orozco standing next to a car; his stereo was wrapped in cloth on top of the car. Loeza grabbed the stereo and was walking back to his car when Orozco stabbed him in the back with a six- to eight-inch knife. The knife punctured a lung, and he needed surgery. Loeza was interviewed by detectives, and he identified Orozco as the person who stabbed him. Charges were filed, but the case against Orozco was dismissed when Loeza was afraid to come to court.

3. Fidel Arce was called as a witness on March 27, 2007. He was a quadriplegic confined to a wheelchair and used a machine to assist his breathing. He testified that on March 18, 2004, he was seventeen-years-of-age and had lived in Hawaiian Gardens his entire life. He was a member of the Varrio Hawaiian Gardens gang. At the time, his girlfriend was five months pregnant and later gave birth to his son.

4. On March 18, 2004, he was consuming large amounts of drugs and alcohol with other members of the VHG gang, including Sordo and Sepe (Jose Orozco). They decided to commit a drive-by shooting of rival gang members. Sordo gave him a gun; and he, Sordo, and Sepe got into a car. Sordo was driving, and Arce sat in the front passenger seat. Sepe was the only other occupant in the car, and was sitting in the back seat behind Arce.

Arce felt that he was too intoxicated to commit a shooting, and he handed the gun to Sepe in the back seat. The next thing Arce knew, he woke up in the hospital as a quadriplegic. He had suffered a gunshot wound to his head. The bullet was still in his head. [Other testimony established that Arce was thrown from the vehicle after being shot.] No charges were filed against Sepe.

Arce had a difficult time making the decision to come to court to testify. However, neither he nor his family had received any threats from Sepe in this matter. However, he was concerned about his ability to protect his family in his condition.

5. Deputy Andrew Cruz testified that on June 25, 2006, he conducted a contraband search of Jose Orozco's single man jail cell at the Men's Central Jail. He found a razor blade secreted between the cell bars and the concrete slab above the bars. Deputy Cruz further testified that four months later, another razor blade, along with some graffiti, was found in Orozco's cell. Inmates in the section where Orozco was housed were not allowed to have razor blades because they could be affixed to something rigid to make a shank.

Factor C – prior felony convictions

The parties stipulated that Jose Luis Orozco had previously been convicted of an attack on an officer in 2004, second-degree auto burglary in 1996, and ex-felon in possession of a firearm in 1997.

PENALTY PHASE: DEFENSE CASE

The defense presented four witnesses in mitigation during the penalty phase of the trial.

1. Martha Buenrostro was Jose Orozco's teacher in the third grade at Hawaiian Gardens Elementary School. She testified that he was a quiet, well-liked child who kept mostly to himself. He struggled academically, more in language than in math. He had to take English as a Second Language because he spoke only Spanish. He was in the low group of the class academically, but she did not believe that he needed placement in a special education class.

2. Jerry Friedman was Jose Orozco's teacher during the second half of fourth grade and all of sixth grade. Academically, Orozco struggled in most subjects and was usually in the lower third of students, but he did not have any learning disabilities. At the time, Hawaiian Gardens Elementary School did not have the after-school programs to help struggling students. Friedman knew about the VHG gang and had seen some gang graffiti on Orozco's notebooks, but he did not believe that he would join the gang. The school tried to discourage students from joining gangs, but it was difficult. Gang life was enticing to students and glorified by their peers and family members; many of the students were involved with gangs. Friedman could not recall either of Orozco's parents coming to class or to parent-teacher conferences.

3. Juan Carlos Orozco was the older brother of Jose Luis Orozco. He testified that like his brother, he was a member of the VHG gang and that most of his friends were fellow gang members. Jose Orozco's nickname was Sepe. Their father called him Sepe because his hair looked like a famous clown named "Sepenia." According to the witness, it was a family nickname and not a gang moniker.

    Their parents were hardworking, and they both had jobs. The sons hid their gang membership from their parents. Their mother knew about the gang presence in the neighborhood, and she tried to keep the boys out of the gang. Jose was married to Maribel, with whom he had two children. When their parents moved from Hawaiian Gardens to Las Vegas, they were joined by Juan, Jose, and Maribel. However, Maribel was a methamphetamine addict, and she quickly returned to Hawaiian Gardens.

    Jose Orozco had horns tattooed on his head to signify that his wife had cheated on him.

4. Detective Mark Lillienfeld of the Los Angeles County Sheriff's Department was called to testify regarding the shooting of Fidel Arce. He was not the original investigating officer on the case, but he located the car in which Arce stated he was shot. In August 2006, he ordered certain forensic tests to be conducted on the car. A forensic exam of the car was conducted, but no blood or residue was found.

PENALTY PHASE CLOSING ARGUMENTS

On April 2, 2007, the case was argued to the jury on the penalty phase. Deputy District Attorney Lowell Anger presented the prosecution argument that a death sentence was the appropriate punishment for Jose Luis

Orozco. First, he portrayed Jerry Ortiz as a hero who was a great cop, a devoted family man, and a loyal friend.

However, a jury will normally not impose a death sentence unless the defendant has a history of violence and no respect for human life. In this regard prosecutor Anger portrayed Orozco as a predator who was an ideal candidate for the death penalty. The following excerpt from his argument puts this in its proper perspective:

> *What is the appropriate punishment for someone who's not committed one isolated abhorrent out-of-character act of violence in his life, but he's continually chosen to flaunt the rules of decent society and chosen violence? And when he does, he does it as a predator from a position of advantage, and generally from behind. He shot Jerry [Ortiz] from behind a door, he shot Jeffrey Williams and Fidel Arce from behind, and he pistol whipped Paul Camarena when he was trapped in a car.*
>
> *What is the appropriate punishment for someone's legacy of a life of moral failure is so much destruction and pain? (Reporter's transcript, page 2791.)*

Prosecutor Lowell Anger concluded his argument with this powerful message to the jury:

> *And there is no compelling reason to show the defendant any mercy. The proper punishment for the murder of Deputy Ortiz, and for all the defendant's other vicious predatory attacks, is the judgment of death.*
>
> *Please let the defendant know that Jerry's life was not worth more than his own. Thank you. (Reporter's transcript, page 2816.)*

Defense attorney Stanley Perlo then argued to the jury on behalf of the defense, asking the jury to spare his client's life and return a verdict of

life imprisonment without the possibility of parole. He argued that Orozco's lifetime of gang membership and drug abuse were mitigating factors
that could not be ignored; the jury should spare him a death sentence.

The jury began its deliberation in the afternoon of April 2, 2007.

PENALTY PHASE VERDICT

On April 3, 2007, the jury returned its verdict of death. The jury announced the verdict at 11:20 a.m. It had reached the verdict of death after
deliberating less than a day.

Judge Philip Hickok thanked the jurors for their service and dismissed them. He set May 3, 2007, as the date for sentencing of the defendant.

SENTENCING

On May 3, 2007, Judge Philip Hickok first denied a defense motion
for a new trial. Then the court denied a defense motion for modification
of the penalty from death to life imprisonment without the possibility of
parole. The court gave the following statement in denying the motion:

> (T)he motion for modification of the penalty from death
> to life imprisonment without the possibility of parole is de-
> nied. It's denied for the following reasons, which I'm going to
> state, and thereafter put in the file.
>
> The first-degree murder of Jerry Ortiz was an intention-
> al killing, personally committed by the defendant Jose Luis
> Orozco. Further, this murder was premeditated, willful, and
> committed with malice aforethought. This cold-blooded, vi-
> cious murder was committed while the victim was acting as a

peace officer engaged in the performance of his duties. The intentional killing was by means of lying in wait. It was done for the purpose of avoiding or preventing a lawful arrest. And, it was committed for the benefit of and in association with a criminal street gang.

Relative to the above, I note the following as far as the circumstances of the crimes of which the defendant was convicted in this trial: prior to the crimes, Orozco twice mentioned if he stayed on in California, he was going to wind up killing a cop or someone; that he wanted to kill a cop; be a mobster; put the Hawaiian Gardens Varrio gang on the map.

On June 20, 2005, Orozco attempted the willful, deliberate, premeditated murder of Jeffrey Williams by personally shooting the victim twice from behind as the victim was trying to run away from him. Then, on June 24, 2005, Orozco murdered Deputy Sheriff Jerry Ortiz, while Deputy Ortiz was searching for the defendant for the previously mentioned attempted murder on June 20. The murder of Jerry Ortiz was committed while the defendant concealed himself behind the front door of a residence in the same neighborhood in which the attempted murder occurred, and in which the defendant was living. The murder was committed without regard to two extremely young and impressionable girls being present in the same room as the execution. Then following the murder, the spent cartridge was expended from the revolver, Orozco attempted to clean the residue from his hands, hid five houses away in a bathtub filled with wet towels, in case tear gas was used. While in custody at the Bellflower courthouse, he told a fellow gang member and associate to arrange to have the witnesses to the murder, including these two young girls, killed so they wouldn't testify. Orozco was an active member of the Hawaiian Gardens Varrio gang, one that openly hated African Americans, and frequently committed crimes of vio-

lence such as murders, shootings, assaults, robberies, witness intimidation, among others. Finally, that after the killing of Deputy Ortiz, the Hawaiian Gardens Varrio gang was openly bragging about the event, and how its stature with the Mexican Mafia would be increased.

In addition, I note the criminal convictions in the file, and criminal activities of the defendant prior to and since his incarceration: The March 18, 2004, cold-blooded shooting of a fellow gang member, Fidel Arce, at point blank range to the back of the head, one that left him a quadriplegic for life. The pistol whipping of Saul Camarena, a neighborhood acquaintance, on October 11, 2002, in front of the defendant's house. The October 18, 2002, stabbing of Gilbert Loeza, an associate, again in the back, not giving the victim an opportunity to defend himself. Then another three felony convictions in 1996, 1997, and 2004, as well as a couple of razor blades discovered concealed in his cell while in custody.

I'm also compelled at this time to point out the impact of the loss of Jerry Ortiz has had on his family, his co-workers, and the community at large. Fellow law enforcement officers spoke to the effect of the death of Deputy Ortiz. Deputy Ortiz's widow, two sons, mother and sister also testified during the trial.

I've carefully considered every possible mitigating factor, and all mitigating evidence, including but not limited to the testimony of Orozco's elementary school teachers and his brother in describing his life leading to this killing. I've also considered the defendant's drug use, and his membership in the Hawaiian Gardens Varrio gang.

I have painstakingly and carefully weighed and considered the aggravating and mitigating factors as set forth in Penal Code section 190.3, and I find the aggravating circumstances are so substantial in comparison with the mitigating *circumstances that it absolutely warrants death instead of life without parole.*

These reasons for the denial of the application for modification are ordered to be entered in the clerk's minute orders pursuant to Penal Code section 190.4 (E). (Reporter's transcript, pages 2865-2868.)

Before the court rendered sentence, Chela Ortiz, the slain deputy's widow, made a statement in open court. She addressed Jose Orozco directly as she read a letter written by her stepson, Jeremy Ortiz. "Why did you do it? Why did you have to hide behind a door like a coward and shoot an unsuspecting man? If you had faced my dad like a man, you would have not stood a chance. You look like a scared rat. I feel sorry for your children, knowing that your dad will be on death row. Along with the ugly horns on your head, you will be going to hell . . ."

After reading the letter, Chela Ortiz made her own statement. She stated in part:

> *You took away my husband, way too soon. You took him away from all of us, and it has been devastating. But I want you to know that you did not break our family. We have love and support that you will never understand. And our Jerry is in heaven, and we will see him again. ... Jerry was a beautiful man in every single way. His memory will live on as a loving father, a wonderful brother, and amazing husband, and a giving son. And you will always be remembered as a coward. Jerry Ortiz. 62405. Thank you. (Reporter's transcript, pages 2869-2870.)*

Judge Hickok then pronounced judgment and sentence, stating in part that:

"...it is now the order of this court that you shall suffer the death penalty, that said penalty to be inflicted within the walls of the state prison at San Quentin, California, in the manner prescribed by law and at a time to be fixed by this court in the warrant of execution."

(Reporter's transcript, page 2871.)

COMMENTARY OF STEVE COOLEY

The criminal history of Jose Luis Orozco illustrates a failure in the criminal justice system. Orozco had committed a series of violent crimes for which he was not convicted because the victims were afraid to come to court to testify. One of the victims was a quadriplegic who was shot in the head at close range by Orozco. There is a gang subculture that sends a message that victims and witnesses who testify against gang members are putting themselves and their families in jeopardy. Without the testimony of these civilian witnesses, many serious cases involving gang members cannot be successfully prosecuted.

The Los Angeles County District Attorney's Office has a witness relocation program in which civilian witnesses in gang cases are relocated to residences far from the gang territory where the crime was committed. This provides a substantial degree of protection to the witness. Many serious cases against gang members have been successfully prosecuted because a courageous and conscientious witness was relocated and was no longer threatened or intimidated by the neighborhood gang.

LESSONS LEARNED

The murder of Deputy Jerry Ortiz was truly a cowardly act by a violent gang member who hid behind a door and shot the unsuspecting deputy.

There are several lessons to be learned from this tragedy.

Looking for a violent felon who had shot somebody requires more than one officer. Even though deputies are often deployed alone (as was Deputy Ortiz), he was actively looking for Orozco who was known to be armed and dangerous. With hindsight, it can be seen that pairing up with another deputy (even if they continued to drive separate patrol cars) would have been a safer approach while looking for Orozco.

In addition, the deputy apparently did not communicate with the dispatcher and other deputies when he saw Orozco. He chased him alone and knocked on doors to try to find him. This is a tragic (but classic) example of "Tombstone Courage," one of the ten deadly officer-safety errors described by the legendary Pierce Brooks in his book, ...officer down, code three. (Still worth the read more than forty years later, the book is available from several sources by typing the title in your search engine.)

Supervisors and peer officers often reflect after tragedies like this, that "everybody knew" this officer's work habits including ignoring policy and training and needlessly putting himself/herself into dangerous situations (or not wearing a seatbelt, or overdriving, or unnecessarily cursing at people. . .or any number of things that could be prevented by appropriate supervision and peer pressure).

The importance of guiding, training, and caring enough to provide correction when warranted would go a long way toward reducing these kinds of tragedies in our profession.

Deputy Jerry Ortiz

Date of birth: September 16, 1969
Date appointed: February 9, 1990
End of watch: June 24, 2005

Jerry and Chela Ortiz were married on May 28, 2005, just three weeks before his murder

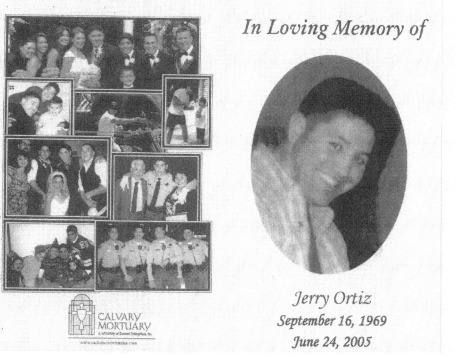

In Loving Memory of

Jerry Ortiz
September 16, 1969
June 24, 2005

CALVARY
MORTUARY

Program with family photographs distributed at funeral services for Jerry Ortiz

**The front door at 12215 East 223rd Street
where Deputy Ortiz was shot**

Jose Luiz Orozco AKA "Sepe"

- Varrio Hawaiian Gardens gang member
- Horns tattooed on his forehead

**Orozco was arrested hiding in this bathtub at
12239 East 223rd Street**

The murder weapon, a .38 caliber Taurus revolver, was found in a cardboard box at 12239 East 223rd Street

Jerry Ortiz was a boxer on the sheriff's boxing team. The Jerry Ortiz Memorial
Boxing & Youth Fitness Gym in El Monte was established in his honor

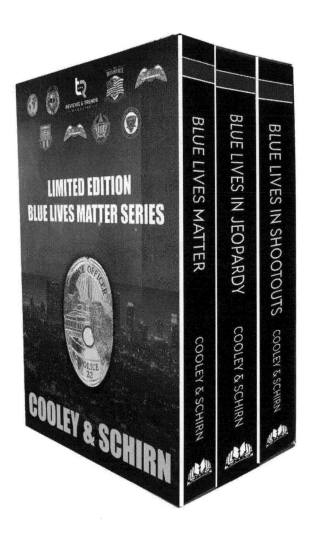

The final book of the *Blue Lives* trilogy
will be released in the fall of 2019.
Blue Lives Under Fire - Shootouts
Visit www.bluelivesmatterbook.com
for more information.

Made in the USA
Las Vegas, NV
09 February 2021

17576896R00149